MORAL
NOTIONS

STUDIES IN
PHILOSOPHICAL PSYCHOLOGY

Edited by
R. F. HOLLAND

MORAL
NOTIONS

by

JULIUS KOVESI

LONDON
ROUTLEDGE & KEGAN PAUL
NEW YORK: HUMANITIES PRESS

First published 1967
by Routledge & Kegan Paul Ltd
Broadway House, 68–74 Carter Lane
London, E.C.4

Printed in Great Britain
by C. Tinling & Co. Ltd,
Liverpool, London and Prescot

CONTENTS

PREFACE

SINCE I have been talking about the ideas expressed in this study for several years on formal and informal occasions, there are a great number of people who helped me in shaping them. Some may not even be aware that they did so. They range in place and time from some of the undergraduates at Balliol during the years 1956–58, to some of my present colleagues in Australia. That I cannot mention them all here does not mean that I have forgotten how much I owe them. But I must express my special gratitude to Professor S. A. Grave, to Mr. Roy Holland and to my wife. Professor Grave read through an earlier version of my script, then with equal patience scrutinized the present one, and he was always ready to help me make my views clearer. For the views and the remaining obscurities he is not of course responsible. My editor helped not only with many valuable suggestions but with his patience and kind encouragement. My wife's help can be illustrated by this typical dialogue:

Me: 'I know it sounds much better the way you put it but that's not what I want to say'.

She: 'Whatever you want to say, you cannot say it like that'.

If sometimes I was forced to say it like that after all, I apologize to the reader.

CHAPTER ONE

BETWEEN GOOD AND YELLOW

1. MATERIAL AND FORMAL ELEMENTS

'GOOD' is not like 'yellow'. Evaluative terms are not like descriptive terms. We should not assume, however, that the difference between 'good' and 'yellow' is the same sort of difference as the one between evaluative terms and descriptive terms.

There have been many arguments in this century over the difference between 'good' and 'yellow'. They are obviously different, and these arguments were not designed merely to demonstrate the obvious: sometimes the simple difference between these two words was used to illustrate or to introduce us to the far more complex and sophisticated difference between evaluative and descriptive terms, but more often it was simply assumed that to demonstrate the difference between these two words is at the same time to explain the other complex difference.

'Yellow' is not a typical descriptive word. It is a typical colour-word and colour-words have special features of their own. Neither is 'good' a typical evaluative word, it is the most general word of com-

1

mendation. Not only the word 'good', but practically every word in our language, including descriptive terms, is unlike simple colour-words. And not only the word 'yellow', but practically every word in our language, including evaluative terms, is unlike the most general word of commendation.

I intend to show why and how simple colour-words have special features of their own by contrasting colour-words with the rest of our vocabulary. The difference that we shall find between 'yellow', and, say, 'table' is the same sort of difference that some moral philosophers find between 'yellow' and 'good'. I am not trying to eliminate thereby the distinction between evaluation and description. Rather in order to indicate where that distinction lies I have to begin by showing that it does not lie in the simple difference between 'good' and 'yellow'. For if we want to find *at the same time* and by the same arguments the difference between 'yellow' and 'good' *and* the difference between descriptive and evaluative terms, we are bound to be mistaken in our attempts to draw both these distinctions.

Tables are a great stumbling-block to philosophers. Some say that we just perceive that the object in front of us is a table. Others, with justification, object to this by saying that all that we perceive are qualities given to our senses, the hardness, smoothness and the colour of the object: there is no quality of *being-a-table* as such that we could perceive; we construct— they say—our notion of a table out of empirically-given qualities. It is true there is no perceivable quality called 'tableness' as there is a perceivable quality called 'yellow'. But there is no reason whatsoever to say that therefore we construct our notion of table out of perceivable qualities. This is not the case either historically or logically. Historically, without a need for tables we would not have these pieces of furniture; logically, we cannot understand the notion of a table without understanding that need.

Owing to the construction of our body, and due to some social conventions, we find it convenient to sit by bending our knees at something like a right angle. So sitting, our bodies are at a certain height. If we want to write or place cups and other objects within our reach, we need to have flat surfaces at a convenient height relative to our position when sitting. So we manufacture pieces of furniture that meet these needs. These pieces of furniture which we call tables may have different shapes and may be constructed in various ways, but as long as they meet these needs in an accepted way we are entitled to call them '*tables*'.

Certain qualities must be present in a piece of furniture in order that we should be able to call it a '*table*', but there is no strict rule as to what these qualities must be. There are various ways of making tables, and we can use various materials. On the other hand not just anything will qualify as a table. Our reasons for having tables constitute, as it were, the guiding principle for deciding what are tables and what are not, or what new constructions will be accepted as tables.

I would like to introduce here two technical terms borrowed from Aristotle, form and matter. By introducing these terms I am not going to introduce any metaphysical entities. They are no more mysterious than, say, the terms 'evaluative meaning' and 'des-

3

criptive meaning' employed by contemporary moral philosophers, and I hope they will be more useful. By *matter* I do not mean simply the tangible material of the object, nor by *form* its shape or appearance. In the case of tables, I call the *matter* not only the various materials out of which we may construct tables but any characteristics in which the object may vary without ceasing to be a table. So the shape of the table, far from being its *form* will be part of its matter, since it may change—a table may be oblong, round or square—while the object remains a table. Similarly, whether the object has four legs or three, whether it is made of wood or iron, are questions about the material elements of tables.

The very fact that the material elements are un-specified and may vary, calls for the introduction of the term *form*. An answer to the question why we call a large variety of objects 'tables' and refuse the word to other objects gives what I want to call the *form* of a table.

I intend to use these terms not only when we analyse our notions of objects but also in our analysis of human actions. We can commit murder in a great variety of ways. It is the material element of an act of murder that someone drives a knife into his victim's heart, or administers poison, or strangles him, or pushes him over a cliff. Human ingenuity may increase this list, and we may never be able to give a complete enumeration of the ways one can murder someone. What makes all these pieces of human behaviour into acts of murder is what I call the *form* of murder, i.e. that we intentionally take the life of someone who is innocent, with the aim of personal gain or satisfaction.

I do not want to say that, in contrast to the unspecified material element, the formal element is always something final and definable. It is difficult to give precisely once and for all the formal element not only in the case of notions like murder but also in cases like the table. With changes in our needs and social conventions our reasons for having tables might also change and consequently what will count as a table and what will not, will also change. The difference between our notion of a table and that of the Romans for instance, is a difference in the formal element of the respective notions. We could characterize this difference by the phrase 'inverted commas use', a phrase with which we are familiar in contemporary moral philosophy. Disregarding anachronism, the word 'table', with our formal element, could not have played a role in the life of the Romans, except as a descriptive phrase in an inverted commas sense: 'This is what some people in some parts of the world call "table".'

We may be able to see better the need for introducing these technical terms into our analysis of the world we live in and talk about if we contrast the majority of our words with simple words like colour words.

An object may be yellow because we so painted it. We may scrape off this paint and put on another coat, say, a coat of red. In these cases there is no connection between the colour of an object and its other properties. One box may be painted red and another yellow, while all their other properties and features remain the same, and we might call both of them 'letter boxes'.

There are cases where there is a connection between the colour of a thing and its other properties. There is a connection between certain chemical properties of a

leaf and its colour, or between the physical properties
of a prism and its colours. But these are contingent
empirical connections. There is a connection that we
do *not* find between the colour of an object and its
other properties: we never *call* an object 'red' or 'blue'
because of the presence of some other properties in
that object. There is a recognizable quality called
'yellow' and the presence of that very quality entitles
us to say that the object in question is yellow. Though
a follower of Wittgenstein might rightly say that even
the naming of a colour and the subsequent use of that
colour-word involves the existence of a way of life
where there is a need for talking about colours and a
language in which there is a place for colour-words,
this does not affect my present argument.

The important point is that in order for us to judge
something to be yellow, that very quality has to be
present that we have agreed to call by the word
'yellow'. But for us to judge something to be a table
an unspecified group of properties and qualities have
to be present, none of which is that property or quality
that we have agreed to call 'table'. I am not making
the obvious point that a table is not a property or a
quality. I am making a logical rather than an onto-
logical point. When this difference between colour-
words and 'table' which I am now pointing to was
noticed as between colour-words and 'good', the term
'supervenient quality (or property)' or 'consequential
quality (or property)' was suggested to characterize
goodness. But this means that goodness is not a
quality or property at all—for the same sort of reason
as table is not a quality or property. We remember the
familiar argument which says that while it is possible

for two objects to differ only in their colour, it is impossible to say that two objects are exactly the same in every respect except in this, that one is good and the other is not. If one is good and the other is not, then they must differ in some recognizable respect. What they must differ in, however, is not what we call goodness.

But by showing this difference between 'good' and 'yellow' we have not at the same time contrived to throw light upon a characteristic feature of evaluative terms. It is equally impossible to say that two pieces of furniture are exactly the same in every respect except in this, that one is a table and the other is not. This is so because, over and above or beside the unspecified material elements that need to be present in order that an object may qualify as a table, there is no extra quality, *being-a-table*, which may be present in one object but not in the other. On the other hand two objects may be exactly the same in every respect except that one is yellow and the other is not. This is so because, as we have seen, we do not say that an object is yellow by virtue of some other qualities in that object, but because of the presence of that very quality we call 'yellow'.

2. LACK OF ENTAILMENT BETWEEN MATERIAL AND FORMAL ELEMENTS

Let us turn now to another aspect of the contrast between colour-words and the word 'good'. I emphasized earlier that the material elements are unspecified. We cannot give a complete enumeration of the conditions that must be fulfilled for the proper use of a term.

Not because of the indefinite number of these conditions, but because these conditions have an open texture. Nor can it be stated how many of these conditions must be present and how many may be absent. For this reason there can be no entailment relation between the material elements and what we say the thing or action is. It cannot be *deduced* from, nor can it be *defined in terms of* the material elements, and this is perhaps one of the secrets that anti-naturalists are after.

There is of course a more respectable sense of definition, when, without reference to material elements, we give what I call the formal element of a notion, when we say what makes the thing what it is. A definition in this sense will determine what material elements we can or cannot accept as constituting the thing. In this sense a definition also functions somewhat like a standard or norm. But both naturalists and anti-naturalists tend to concentrate on a sense of 'definition' in which 'definition' is defining *in terms of* what I call the material elements.

The reasons why we cannot define what a thing or act is in terms of their material elements, or why we cannot make valid deductive arguments where the premisses contain only material elements and the conclusion tells what the thing or act is, is not a special characteristic of evaluative arguments. It has to do with the fact that the sort of things that can constitute a thing or act, their material elements, cannot be enumerated in a final list. It is their formal element which will determine what they are, not a list of their material elements.

In the same way as when we contrast the word

'yellow' with the word 'good' we are not contrasting descriptive with evaluative words but colour-words with the word 'good', when we contrast the word 'rectangular' with the word 'good' we are not contrasting descriptive with evaluative words but geometrical terms with the word 'good'. Colour-words and geometrical terms have features of their own, which, far from being representative of descriptive terms, contrast with them in the same way as they contrast with evaluative terms.

Thus, for instance, Mr. Hare after noting that the proper use of the word 'good' depends on the presence of other qualities—as indeed does the proper use of most of our words—goes on to say: 'We have to inquire, then, whether there is any characteristic or group of characteristics which is related to the characteristic of being good in the same way as the angle-measurements of figures are related to their rectangularity.' (*The Language of Morals*, p. 82.) This contrast, however, cannot illustrate the difference between evaluative and descriptive terms but only the difference between most of our vocabulary and geometrical terms. We have seen that, similarly, there is no group of characteristics which are related to our notion of a table in the same way as the angle-measurements of figures *are* related to their rectangularity. This is so because in geometry there are no open textures.

In one, but an important sense, colour-words function more like the words used in geometry than like ordinary object words such as 'table'. I am not making the absurd suggestion that there is an entailment relation between something being yellow and the

9

judgment that it is yellow, as there is between certain angle measurements and rectangularity. I am comparing them in this respect, that there is no 'gap' between something being yellow and the judgment 'this is yellow' as there is none between certain angle measurements and rectangularity. The entailment relation in the case of geometrical notions is just a sub-class of the reason why there are no 'gaps' in these cases; we are quite sure in these cases what has to be present for us to judge something, such and such. By a 'gap' I mean that we do not move with such ease from observing that something has four or five legs and a flat, square or round surface on it, to the judgment that 'this is a table': or from observing that someone has been administered arsenic or been pierced by a knife, to the judgment 'this is murder', as we move from observing that something is yellow to the judgment 'this is yellow': or from observing that something has certain angle measurements to 'this is rectangular'. Colours can shade into other colours, but this is not the same as having an open texture in the sense in which I want to say that the concept of a table has an open texture. The concept of a table has an open texture not because tables can shade into other pieces of furniture, but because even the unmistakable tables can be made in a variety of ways and manners.

It is interesting to observe what different treatment this 'gap' receives in the case of material objects and in the case of actions. In the case of material objects the problem is usually treated as part of the theory of knowledge. Here the talk is seldom of inferences but rather of 'constructions': how do we construct material objects out of what is given to the senses? In the case of actions not only are philosophers more prone to talk about inferences, but various other considerations confuse the issue. The most important of these is that the problem of description and evaluation has been telescoped into the problem of what is given to the senses and what we judge the action to be. Sometimes we are led to believe that the difference between description and evaluation is to be found in the difference between what is given to the senses and what we judge an action to be, and we are asked then to justify an inference in moving from the one to the other. There are problems in justifying an evaluative judgment after having made several descriptive statements, and there might even be problems connected with inference-procedures here. What I am trying to point out now is that these should not be confused, as they often are, with the problem of the connections between what is given to the senses and what we judge a thing or act to be. *This* problem presents itself in the same way in the case of both descriptive and evaluative terms.

We have seen the lack of entailment relationship between what I call the material and formal elements of our concepts; we shall see later how pointless it is to try to bridge this gap by creating a major premise in order to *have* an entailment relation. Yet this is what some moral philosophers are trying to do. As if we could solve *the* problem of epistemology by the following way: 'There are two sorts of statements that we can make about a piece of furniture: examples of the first sort are, "This piece of furniture has four legs and a flat surface", "This has such-and-such a height": examples of the second sort are, "This is a table", "This is a desk"; the first sort of remark is usually given as a reason for making the second sort of remark, but the first sort does not by itself entail the second sort, nor vice versa. Yet there seems to be some close logical connection between them. Our problem is: what is this connection? What we need is a major premise: whatever has four legs and a flat surface and has such-and-such a height is a table. Then we can proceed: this has . . . , therefore this is a table.'

To talk about deducing or even inferring that something is a table sounds strange, and yet in a different field many moral philosophers give this strange treatment to the same type of problem. I have been trying to suggest why they do this. It has not been observed that the 'gap' between what is given to our senses and what we claim an act or thing to be exists in the case of both descriptive *and* evaluative terms. Instead, this 'gap' has been construed as the 'gap' between description and evaluation, and then by choosing simple words like colour-words as examples of descriptive words, and more complex words as examples of evaluative words, philosophers have given us the impression that the difference between description and evaluation is to be found in the difference between what is given to the senses and what we say a thing or action is. Further, if we superimpose on this the idea that the problem of evaluation is somehow a problem of deductive arguments, then we have arrived at the strange situation that I have just observed: in the case of material objects, where the field is free from the moral philosophers' preoccupation with deductive arguments, our 'gap' remains a problem of the theory of knowledge; but in the field of evaluative terms the same 'gap' is required to be bridged by an inference.

3. THE DIFFERENCE IN MORAL AND OTHER NOTIONS IS A DIFFERENCE IN THE FORMAL ELEMENTS

I want to say that 'driving', 'shopping', 'having a bath', 'gardening', 'writing' are not moral notions, while 'lying', 'revenge', 'inadvertence', 'cheating' are. Both groups of notions can be analysed into their formal and material elements as I use these technical terms. My object in showing this is *not* to eliminate the difference between what is usually called 'evaluation' and 'description', or the difference between moral and other notions. There is such a difference, but it is not the same as the difference which holds between the material and formal elements of a notion. We find this difference between *different formal elements*, between different notions. In the case of moral as well as other notions we bring together an unspecified group of features, aspects or qualities of things, situations or objects. But the *point* of collocating these features, aspects or qualities, the reason for grouping them together, is different. There are not only moral and non-moral points or reasons for forming our notions but a great number of others, and it is among these that the oversimplified distinction between moral and non-moral notions is to be found.

In describing the way we came to have tables I began by referring to the physiological and sociological reasons for the way we sit, and then referred to the need for having flat surfaces relative to our height when sitting. This is a partial description of our reason for having tables which is essential to the understanding of our notion of a table. A complete account of the behaviour and life of this notion would also include, among other things, that we want to manufacture these objects, buy them and sell them, remove them and identify them. I would like to draw here a useful parallel with the word 'lever' suggested to me by the late Professor J. L. Austin. Before people thought of manufacturing levers one didn't go to a special shop to get them but one asked for a lever from anyone likely to have the sort of object that would do the job. What was or was not a lever then depended solely on what did or did not fulfil the function of lifting objects in a particular manner. But once levers came on the market the situation was different. If one asks in a hardware shop for a lever now, the assistant cannot go out into his backyard and look for any piece of metal that would do the job. Manufacturing, buying and selling, introduced new criteria for what will or will not be accepted as levers. (Perhaps the word 'wrapper' is going through a similar sort of change at present.) Similarly the fact that established firms manufacture tables, that we buy and sell according to rules partly determines what will and will not be a table. Another important activity in our way of life is the writing of inventories and that articles of furniture very often have to feature on such inventories is a further element influencing the life of such notions as 'table'. It should not be surprising then that if we want to give an inventory of a house or describe precisely what is in a house or a room, the word 'table' admirably fits our purpose in our activity of describing. We do not only use tables, we also use the word 'table'. And because we do not only want to write or eat on tables but want to sell them or identify them and list them on inventories the life and use of the word 'table' is shaped by all these various activities; that is, the life and use of the word 'table' is shaped not only by the way we use the object table, but also by all those other activities in the performance of which we have to use the word 'table'.

If, on the other hand, the point of having a term in our language is not that we want to identify, buy and sell something but because we want to avoid or promote something, excuse or blame people for certain happenings or acts, then we have a different type of formal element shaping the life and use of our term. It is in this field that the difference between different types of notions is to be found.

4. THE FORMAL AND NOT THE MATERIAL ELEMENT MAKES A THING OR ACT TO BE WHAT IT IS

Let us now consider the notion of an inadvertent act. Cavemen not only did not have tables, but at some stage they did not have the notion of an inadvertent act. So when one of them knocked the water over the campfire while putting on the wood he no doubt received rough treatment from his fellows. It was with the realization that we are not responsible for all happenings that are caused by the movement of our bodies that we must have started forming the notion of an inadvertent act. Just as if we had not needed flat surfaces relative to our height when sitting we would not have begun to form the notion of a table, and thus have started manufacturing them, so if we had not had the need to blame or excuse ourselves

15

and others, we would not have begun to form the notion of an inadvertent act, and thus have started excusing ourselves and others.

When I reach for the salt I have to move my arm. If while moving my arm my elbow happens to pass through the space occupied by a teapot and the impact knocks it over either I was clumsy or I did it inadvertently. If the teapot was within the range of objects that I might reasonably be expected to notice, then I was clumsy. In both cases I want to claim that knocking over the teapot was *not* the object of my exercise. We have come to realize that in performing an act we have to make certain movements or changes in our environment (not always as simple as the movement of an arm; we can not only break cups but also romances inadvertently) and in doing so the movements may produce by-products.

One day I inadvertently break a teapot while reaching for the salt. Another day I am walking on the beach and I jump back from a sudden wave. In so doing I destroy a sandcastle, inadvertently. There is no observable similarity between the two inadvertent acts, and if we were to think of a third example we would not conduct our search for it with observable similarities in mind; we would look for cases which however empirically dissimilar, would nevertheless *come to the same thing.* Now the various ways in which we can perform inadvertent acts constitute what I call the material elements of inadvertency. Inadvertency is not an extra element over and above our doing what we do, it is what these various doings all amount to. The formal element is *that* same thing they all come to. Without this formal element we would be unable to find new examples of inadvertent acts, and unable to follow a rule in using the term. We must recognize what it is for an act to be inadvertent, no matter what else it may be, before we can call it 'inadvertent', and it is *this* recognition, and not the recognition of any empirical similarities between different instances of inadvertent acts which enables us to follow a rule in using this term.

Tables are, of course, similar to each other; but we did not arrive at our notion of a table by having discovered similarities between some of our pieces of furniture. Rather, we make them similar because, only by being made more or less similar, can they meet the need that tables were invented to meet. But the number of ways in which we can do something inadvertently is not so limited. Our police force would have a much easier job if, for instance, the number of ways in which we could commit murder were limited to a few standard techniques. On the other hand one could not get away with murder by claiming that our new method of putting an end to someone's life had no similarity at all with all the previous hitherto recorded cases of murder. We could not conduct our defence by showing differences in the material elements, but only by showing differences in the formal elements: that is, by showing that it was not intentional, or that I had a legal right to kill, etc. (We have to observe, however, that as manufacturing or stocktaking have standardized tables, so the law has standardized some of our moral notions.)

When Hume asked us to 'take any action allowed to be vicious; wilful murder, for instance', he asked us in effect to examine what I call its material elements.

(*Treatise*, Book III, Part I, Section I.) Of course, he was right in saying that we cannot find that 'matter of fact or real existence' which we call vice. But before we get to virtue and vice let us observe that Hume on his own ground should not be able to find that matter of fact or real existence that we call murder either. He should not have asked us to take wilful murder as an illustration of a state of affairs that we can perceive and describe in his sense of 'description'. To see the real nature of Hume's claim we might take as our example a man who is pushing a length of sharp steel attached to a piece of wood into the space occupied by another man in circumstances that we constantly associate with the collapse of the other man shortly afterwards. We could take as another example a man on a very high cliff pushing over another man in circumstances that we constantly associate with the other man's falling down, and in turn when this is constantly associated with the man remaining permanently motionless. We cannot but agree that not only is vice not a matter of fact or real existence that we can observe, but that murder likewise is not a perceivable object in the world, nor does it consist of perceivable relationships between objects. The conclusion from this, however, is *not* that therefore virtue and vice, murder or kindness are not the objects of our reason. Rather, what follows from this is simply that they are not the objects of our senses. They *are* the object of our reason. The distinction is all important and we must beware of Hume's systematic confusion of perceiving and knowing. He ends this Section by saying: 'let us see that the distinction of virtue and vice is not founded merely on the relations of objects, nor is perceived by reason'; but one should not talk like this. We do *not* perceive with our reason any more than we know with our fingers; though we might use this phrase very figuratively as we might also say that we have the truth at our fingertips.

I am not saying that there are two sorts of objects, objects of sense and objects of reason, and that murder and vice belong to the latter category. I am not arguing over the inventory of the universe. It was G. E. Moore's solution in a similar predicament to increase the number of objects in the universe by one, and then call it 'good'. Hume's solution was to turn somewhere else (into his own breast) where he could perceive or introspect something, because he thought that this was the sort of thing knowledge was or ought to be. I am simply saying that knowing is different from perceiving, and we do not perceive something called murder; we know that certain acts are acts of murder in the same way as we know that certain objects are tables. We do not perceive something called 'table' over and above the material elements that have to be present in order that something should be a table. In an important sense, in the world there *is* no value and there are no murders, tables, houses, accidents or inadvertent acts. But our language is not about *that* world in which there is no value or no tables, houses, accidents or inadvertent acts. That world, the world of raw data, cannot be described for the sense of that world also lies outside it and the very description of it, likewise, lies outside it. Thereof one really cannot speak. In our language the nearest analogy to the words that would mirror the world of data are colour words, so I am not criticizing Hume alone here, but also those moral philosophers who do not use the word 'descriptive' itself descriptively, but as a standard to which some terms or statements are expected to conform, and who regard colour words as the nearest examples of this ideal standard.

5. THE FORMAL AND NOT THE MATERIAL ELEMENT ENABLES US TO FOLLOW A RULE

Whatever might be the advantages of constructing a language that would mirror the world of data, our language functions differently from such a language. In our language, to be able to understand the significance or the meaning of a term, we have to be able to follow a rule in using that term, not to be able to perceive an entity of which our term is a name. We have just seen that 'murder' is not the name of an observable happening nor of any of its constituents. Let us rather see what it was that enabled us to take two happenings, pushing a knife into someone and pushing someone over a cliff, as examples of the same thing. What enabled us to follow a rule here? As in the case of inadvertent acts, if we were to think of a third example of murder we would not seek empirical similarities.

The fact that in each case of murder someone's life is terminated is not a sufficient similarity, though this element must be there to turn an attempted murder into murder. But it is also present in the case of natural death, or accidental killing, or when we kill someone inadvertently. Moreover, examples of murder are *acts* on the part of the person who was not killed: the word 'attempted' does not qualify the death of a person but the success of the act intended by someone else. In order for an act to be an act of murder, and in order for it to be distinguishable from other acts that result in the death of a person, other features or aspects of an act must be present and/or absent. As we selected certain features that have to be present for an act to be inadvertent, because we recognized that the presence of these should excuse someone—and we need excusing; so we selected certain features that need to be present for an act to be an act of murder, because we recognized that the presence of these would render someone liable to blame—and we need to blame and to discourage certain sorts of act. There are of course other notions of acts which have excusing or blaming as their formal element, like mistake and accident on the one hand and cruelty and robbery on the other. This leads us to a hierarchy of material and formal elements. As various movements are the material elements of various acts of murder, so murder itself, along with cruelty, robbery and so on, are material elements of vice. The number of ways in which we can be vicious is not limited. Some of the material elements of the notion of vice are already formed by us into notions consisting of formal and material elements, like murder. We should not suppose that the proper use of our words depends on the presence or absence or configurations of simple qualities in the world; or that our whole vocabulary is, as it were, only one level above such simple words as colour words. It is not necessarily qualities or properties or movements that need to be present for the proper use of a word; we may have to state what needs to be present by a word which already functions in such a way that for *its* proper use other things must be present. Further, it is not only qualities and properties and movements that we have to mention in this context, but also features and aspects of situations and things, intentions and expectations, or perhaps some aspect of a legal, scientific or other conceptual framework. Empirically observable qualities, properties or movements do not take precedence in this list. So if Hume could not find 'that matter of fact, or real existence, which you call *vice*' it should not surprise us.

When I claim that we do not need to look for empirical similarities between various instances of the same thing or same act in order to explain why they are instances of the same, I am suggesting something more radical than what I understand Wittgenstein to be suggesting when he said that we find a 'family resemblance' among the various instances or examples of the same thing. He is still looking for empirical similarities between A and Z though it is not one thread that runs from A to Z. A, B and C are connected by one similarity, B, C and D by another and so A is linked to Z though they do not look alike at all. The similarities are connected like threads in a rope. The family resemblances between various games illustrate this picture well. But I do not see any foundation for a claim that we call both football and chess games because football is played with a ball, and so is tennis, while tennis is played by two people, and so is chess. Not only is this insufficient to explain that connection between football and chess which makes both of them games but this way we could connect everything to everything else. We could turn off at a tangent at any similarity and what we would get in the end would not be a rope but a mesh. Balls—cannonballs—were used to bombard cities, and duelling is a matter for two people. What we need in order to understand the notion of a game or the notion of murder is what I call the formal element. This is what enables us to follow a rule. I said that murder is the object of our reason— the phrase is Hume's, and not of my own choosing— not only because we do not find *empirical* similarities between various instances of murder, but because the very activity of following a rule is a rational activity. Since the phrase 'object of reason' makes one reach for Ockam's razor one should also beware of saying that we do not know particulars but universals. What should be said is that we know what this object is only in so far as we know that this is the same as that, and that and that. If I could not follow a rule I would not know what 'it' was, though in suitable conditions I might be able to perceive 'it', or I might be acquainted with 'it'. Now, unless I understood that the two instances I cited as examples of murder are examples of the same thing, I would not know that they were murders however long I stared at each of them. Nor could I understand that they were examples of the same thing unless I could understand *why* they were, and only when I could understand why they were could I follow a rule in looking for new examples.

6. THE UNITY OF FORMAL AND MATERIAL ELEMENTS

We must see therefore that the material and formal elements of a notion are inseparable. This is part of the reason why I introduced these terms instead of talking about two levels or strata of language, or two different language games, because, in these latter phrases, there is no suggestion of inseparable connections between two strata or games. Matter and form are *one pair* of concepts. Without the formal element there is just no sense in selecting, out of many others, those features of a thing or an act that constitute it that thing or act. Not only is there no sense in selecting those features, but some of those features simply would not exist at all, e.g. in the case of inadvertent acts there just would not be a by-product of an act. Out of the stream of movements that I continually perform we would not pair the reaching for the salt and knocking over the teapot, let alone call the empirically more impressive performance the by-product of the other (especially when it embarrasses me so much that I do not even complete my movement in reaching for the salt). And of course there are innumerable happenings that I also cause to happen when I reach for the salt, some of them even important such as winding my self-winding watch. But we do not wind our self-winding watches inadvertently.

That without the formal element we cannot see the sense of selecting the material elements is especially important in connection with our moral notions. For the contemporary distinction between 'evaluation' and 'description' sometimes assumes that facts just *are* outside in the world waiting for us to recognize them; and that evaluation consists of selecting some facts on 'purely factual grounds' and then expressing our attitude towards them, or making a decision about them. Indeed, decisions and attitudes, insights, wants, needs, aspirations and standards do enter into our moral notions. But they do not enter from the top, they are part and parcel of our notions, and they are organized by the rational activity of concept-formation. Evaluation is not an icing on a cake of hard facts. It is not the case that we have ready-made facts, and that if we want to describe them we state them and say 'yes' about them, and if we want to evaluate them we state them and say 'please' about them. A moral notion does not make a roll-call of facts. There is a point in bringing certain features and aspects of actions and situations together as being relevant, and by removing this point, by removing the 'evaluative element', we are not left with the same facts minus evaluation.

Standards, needs and wants also enter into the formation of terms that we usually call descriptive terms. What makes a term descriptive is not the lack of these but the point of view from which we organize these and other elements into concepts. While in using descriptive terms we have to follow interpersonal rules in a public language to talk about aspects or relationships of the inanimate world—or if we talk about men and animals we do that in so far as they are part of the rest of the world—in using a moral term we have to follow interpersonal rules in a public language to talk about some aspects or relationships of those very beings whose lives are regulated by interpersonal rules. Thus if our subject matter is the relationship of an acorn to an oak tree, as one destroys the other according to the laws of plant physiology and chemistry, not even the strongest attitude of disapproval on our part could turn this into a situation about which we could form a moral notion. Equally if our subject

C

matter were the relationship of a child to his father in the situation where the one kills the other by being blown from the roof and falling on him according to the laws of gravity, by no expression of sentiment towards this unfortunate misadventure could we get the notion of murder out of what happened. Not even if we put a special sort of exclamation mark after the description of what has happened would we get a moral judgment.

On the other hand, except in special circumstances, there is no need to re-emphasize that murder is vicious or wrong, or to say 'this is stealing' in a 'peculiar tone of horror' or write it 'with the addition of some special exclamation marks' (A. J. Ayer: *Language, Truth and Logic*, 2nd ed. p. 107). If someone understands the notion of murder or stealing, to say that they are wrong does not give him any more information. Nevertheless to translate 'wrong' into an exclamation mark is very misleading, for exclamation marks are used for other purposes, and we have a special word that we use to remind ourselves of the point of forming notions like murder, prejudice, cruelty, stealing: we use the word 'wrong'.

But 'good', 'bad', 'right' and 'wrong' are not reminders always. They would always be reminders, but as we shall see not *only* reminders, if all aspects of the world and of situations that can be the subject of moral and other evaluations from the point of view of right and wrong were organized into fully developed notions from these points of view. It is significant that the notions chosen by both Hume and Ayer to illustrate the superfluity of the terms 'vicious' and 'wrong' are such fully-developed moral notions, i.e. 'murder' and 'lying'. In the fourth chapter we shall see an important use of such words as 'good', 'bad', 'right' and 'wrong' when we shall see their use as discriminators. If we did not have the term 'murder' in our language then we would have to describe as killing what we now describe as murder. But instances of killing are a mixed bag from the moral point of view. If we wanted to, as we do want to, discriminate instances of killing from one another from a certain point of view, we would have to say that this killing as against that was wrong. In fact we would want to say that this *type* of killing was wrong, but then we would be well on the way towards the formation of the notion of murder. When we say that this particular killing is wrong or that this *type* of killing is wrong, 'wrong' does not function as a reminder but as a discriminator. When we discriminate between different types of killing, we are not making different evaluations of the same 'descriptive' elements in both. It would be absurd to claim that the only difference between two otherwise identical objects or acts is that we like one but not the other, or that we make different decisions about them. The fact that we like or dislike, or make different decisions about, or express different sentiments towards otherwise identical objects or acts cannot constitute a difference between the objects or the acts. We cannot answer the question: 'Why do we disapprove of one act but not of another though we find no factual difference between the two?' by saying 'Because we express a sentiment of disapproval towards the one but not towards the other'.

We have seen that we cannot say that two objects are exactly the same in every respect except that one is good while the other is not: that they differ only in their goodness. (Let us call this 'argument A'.) Similarly, according to argument A, two acts cannot be the same in every respect except in this, that one of them is right and the other is wrong; nor can we say that two situations are exactly the same except that in one I am under an obligation to do something, but not in the other. There must be some further difference between the two if one is right but the other is wrong, or if in one I am under an obligation but in the other I am not.

We must be very careful to understand the proper significance of argument A and especially to avoid two misuses of this argument.

(1) This argument far from divorcing our evaluative judgments from factual considerations—as it is sometimes assumed to do—rather ties them to such considerations. The assumption that it divorces evaluative judgments from factual considerations could come about this way. Argument A does not apply to colour words. Two objects can be exactly the same in every other respect except that one of them is yellow and the other is not; the colour alone can constitute a difference between two otherwise identical objects. When one object is yellow and the other is not then there is a factual difference between the two objects, namely that one of them is yellow and the other is not. But when one object is good and the other is not, some philosophers are tempted to say that this is not a factual difference between the two objects because, according to argument A, we cannot point to goodness as we can point to yellow as being

present in one object but not in the other. Now to say this is just as strange as to say that while there is a factual difference between a yellow table and a brown table, there is no factual difference between a table and a chair, for while we can point to the presence and absence of the yellow colour in the respective tables we cannot point to the presence and absence of table-ness and chairness in the respective objects.

Argument *A* obviously ties evaluative judgments to factual considerations. If we judge something, *x*, to be good then unless we can point to a relevant (and according to this argument observable) difference in another object, *y*, we must judge *y* to be good also. But not *any* difference would absolve us from judging *y* also good, it must be a relevant difference that *entitles* us to say that *y* is not good. Someone might object that this last sentence does not follow because argument *A* is only a rule of consistency and has nothing to do with *relevant* differences that *entitle* us to judge one thing good and not the other. *Once* we judge something to be good then we have to stick to it and be consistent. We need the factual difference only in order to be able to remember which objects we chose to judge good and also so that, by being able to point to these factual differences, we could teach others how to follow our choices. So if we want to be rational we have to be consistent, otherwise we cannot follow our principles, nor others our advice.

Argument *A* is certainly based on our rationality. But rationality does not begin with our subsequent judgments after we have judged something good, it is even doubtful if we are rational in being consistent if our first judgment was not rational. I said above that if we judged x to be good then we must point to a relevant difference in y if we want to claim that y is not good. Let us reverse the argument and say that if we do not claim that x is good then we must be able to point to a relevant difference in y if we want to claim that y on the other hand *is* good. So argument A applies to our judging something to be good for the first time and not only to our subsequent judgments when we judge everything else which does not differ from y in a relevant respect to be also good. And we may inspect several objects that are different from each other in various different ways and say that none of them are good before we come to the one that we claim to be good. So the difference we must be able to point to cannot be just any difference—there have been differences between the various objects that were not good—but it must be a relevant difference. This leads us to my second point.

(2) Although there must be a factual difference between x and y if x is good and y is not good, it is also the case that there are factual differences among things all of which are good and also among things all of which are bad. Indeed, as we have seen, there may be no empirically similar characteristics between one right act and another or between one wrong act and another. We cannot see what different material elements amount to the same act unless we understand *why* they do so, and unless we understand why they do so we cannot follow a rule in finding further examples.

I objected to the view that the factual difference between good things and bad things serves only the purpose of enabling us to recognize what things we have chosen to judge good or bad and enabling us to teach others how to follow our advice. Now we can object to this view for a more important reason. Since in these cases one cannot follow a rule in using a term by observing empirical similarities, one cannot say: 'things that have such and such empirical similarities I resolve to judge vicious, do so as well'. (Although for safety's sake we might employ this method in cases where we or others are not intelligent enough. We might formulate a rule to our children by saying: 'never touch small white objects like this' while pointing to an aspirin, and then add, in order to avoid the charge of inconsistency: 'except when Daddy gives you one'.) So besides realizing that not just any factual difference will do for the requirements of argument A we must also understand that we do not select these factual differences from the factual point of view. This is how the material and formal elements are inseparable. There must be some differences in the field of material elements between x and y if we want to judge them differently, but we would not know what differences would entitle us to do so without the formal element. All this may sound very cryptic at present and we shall have to elaborate on these points in the following chapters. We shall also see then that it is pointless to ask how we move from the material elements to what we say the thing or action *is* once we realize that we *select* the material elements *because* they constitute that thing or act. There isn't such a thing as murder over and above the various acts that constitute murder. If this gives the impression that the formal element seems superfluous we should re-emphasize the other side of the case and say that the various material elements of a thing or act *are* its material elements only because they constitute the thing or act, because they come to or amount to the same thing or act. This is why we had to introduce the formal element, the point or reason for bringing certain qualities, features or aspects of things, actions or situations together.

Equally, on a higher level of the hierarchy of formal and material elements, 'good', 'bad', 'right' and 'wrong' are not superfluous, and even when they are reminders they are not only or merely reminders. Or rather, when we say 'murder is wrong' it does not merely remind us that murder is murder, but of the reason why such otherwise dissimilar activities as murdering, stealing, lying get into the same class insofar as they are all wrong or vicious. If one is asked what is this point of view, what is the reason for saying that they are all the same, one should refuse to say anything else than that they are wrong, for there is nothing else common to all of them, and to many other possible acts, than that they are wrong. To understand what we mean by saying that they are wrong is to understand what it is which alone is common to all these acts, and the test of whether we understand its meaning is whether we are able to recognize that an empirically different new act also amounts to the same, i.e. that it is also wrong.

7. ELUCIDATION OF MEANING BY ANALOGY

I think Aristotle was right in saying that the way to explain the meaning of the word 'good' is by analogy. Only I do not think he was right in thinking that his theory was a refutation rather than an elucidation of, or possibly an improvement on, Plato's views. (Nic. Eth. 1096 b.[12]) The passage in question—ὡς γὰρ ἐν σώματι ὄψις, ἐν ψυχῇ νοῦς, καὶ ἄλλο δὴ ἐν ἄλλῳ—should not be translated however, as J. A. K. Thomson translates it: 'As sight is good in the body, so is rationality in the mind'. We do not know yet what we mean by saying that sight is *good* in the body. What we want to find out is exactly this: what do we mean by saying that something is good? The way to do this is not by taking one case where we can assume that we know what we mean by it, and then judge everything else good by analogy to this paradigm case: rather, we do it by considering what is common to sight being in the body and intelligence being in the mind. If we cannot see it we should continue: what is rain to the pasture, aspirin for your headache, rest when you are tired? We should have constructions not only with 'in' but also with 'for', 'when', etc., in order to get examples from all the Aristotelian categories. Now, if we stopped and explained why aspirin is on the list we might give the impression that we are explaining the meaning of the word 'medicine' and then one would continue to look for new examples having artificial remedies in mind. Or, if we tried to explain why rest is on the list the person might continue to look for new examples having natural remedies in mind. This is the sort of thing that anti-naturalists rightly object to, namely, substituting for the formal element a statement of some or even a large number of the material elements, even if these elements are not 'natural' as given by nature but already formal elements of lower level notions. We would make the same mistake if we were to say that medicine is a white little pill or a red liquid, or even if we said that it is whatever eliminates headaches.

In making a list of analogies to bring out the meaning of the word 'good', the more divergent our examples the better chance we have of succeeding. Good is the most general and universal formal element in its field. We have seen earlier that the material elements of some of our notions are such that they in turn can be further analysed into formal and material elements. It seems obvious that the higher a term is in this structure the more difficult it is to specify the empirically observable qualities, aspects and relations or movements of things or bodies that have to be present for the proper use of that term.

This does not make these terms vaguer however. We can guess more readily what movements someone must have performed if we know that he misspelled something as against the case when all we know is that he made a mistake. This is so because we can make a mistake in a greater variety of ways: but when we make a mistake what we make is precisely a mistake. We can more readily visualize a road accident than an accident, but we can precisely distinguish between accidents and mistakes. Precision of a term does not depend on the number of ways in which it can be exemplified for the convenience of our perception. We should look for precision in the formal element for the convenience of our rational discourse.

It is not necessarily the case that the higher the term is the more difficult it is to give the material elements on the level just below that term. To take a simple example: it is easier to specify the material elements of a table than of furniture in terms of empirically observable qualities, though it is easy to give examples of the material elements of the notion of furniture, namely tables, chairs and bookcases. Equally it is easier to specify the material elements of murder than of vice in terms of observable movements, though it is easy to give examples of the material elements of vice, namely murder, cruelty, etc.

In cases where we can exemplify something in a greater variety of ways, the more prominent the formal element is; the less variety of examples we can give of a thing, the less prominent the formal element is. Good is a limiting case in its own field. In the case of good, the formal element is so prominent that one is inclined to say that it is just a formal element; something can be 'good' in so many 'empirical' ways. On the other end of the scale something can be yellow only by being yellow. We do not even need to introduce a formal element here, and we can follow a rule in using the word 'yellow' by observing an empirical similarity.

It is true that we point to different objects, to a yellow pillar box, to a yellow canary in teaching how to use the word 'yellow'. As in the case of the explanation of the word 'good', the greater the variety of objects we are pointing to is (though only within one category) the more successful we are in our explanation of how to use the word. But the common feature we find is an empirical quality, and what makes them all yellow is the presence of this very quality. In this case we need the variety of objects to show that the presence of all other qualities is *irrelevant* for the proper use of our word and we must recognize *only one empirical* similarity common to them all. This is quite the reverse process to the explanation of the proper use of the word 'good'.

Between these two limiting cases we find a whole structure of terms and notions organized according to material and formal elements. Here we find, among others, our moral notions. The simple comparison and contrast between 'x is yellow' and 'x is good' obscures this. We should not concentrate our attention so much on 'yellow' and 'good' as on the nature and variety of that 'x'.

CHAPTER TWO

FOLLOWING RULES
AND GIVING REASONS

1. MEANING AND THE FORMAL ELEMENT

AT the beginning of the first chapter we had to introduce what I call the 'formal element' because without it we cannot decide what are and what are not instances of a thing or action. This is so for several connected reasons: we cannot give a list of material elements that would entail what the thing or action is; various instances of things and actions do not resemble each other empirically except in cases where such similarity is required for fulfilling the same function; our terms must be open for hitherto unknown instances of the same thing, and there are always new ways of producing a thing or performing an act. Towards the end of the chapter the same claim was made by saying that, without the formal element, we cannot follow a rule in using a term.

In this chapter we shall investigate some of the implications of this claim. But first I would like to mention further considerations showing that without the formal element we cannot follow a rule in using a term. That this does not seem quite obvious but needs to be substantiated by further arguments, may partly be due to the sort of examples we usually employ to show what 'following a rule' consists of.

At the end of the last chapter we saw that there are certain things that can be exemplified only in one empirically recognizable way: something can be yellow only by being yellow. Plato in the *Republic* (523ff.) takes finger as an example to illustrate the same sort of point: 'Each of them appears equally a finger, and in this respect it makes no difference whether it is observed as intermediate or at either extreme, whether it is white or black, thick or thin, or of any other quality of this kind. For in none of these cases is the soul of most men impelled to question the reason and to ask what in the world is a finger, since the faculty of sight never signifies to it at the same time that the finger is the opposite of a finger.' When Parmenides asks whether hair, mud or dirt have forms (*Parmenides* 130 c.) Socrates replies: 'In these cases, the things are just the things we see; it would surely be too absurd to suppose that they have a Form.' Perhaps it would help to bring out the point I am driving at if I say why I think Plato is mistaken in thinking that the notion of dirt does not involve a formal element. Not only does the notion of dirt imply standards, but unless we understand why we list as examples of dirt custard on a waistcoat and sand on a lens but *not* custard on a plate or sand on the beach we would not know how to continue the list. Unless we understand why the first two are examples of dirt we do not understand what they are examples of, however much custard or sand we have the opportunity of observing.

If we do not use words like 'dirt' but colour words or words like 'finger' to illustrate what is implied in following a rule, we can easily get the impression that we can follow a rule without the formal element. Or we might get the same impression by an often used method of teaching how words acquire meaning. Suppose that a philosopher in a classroom does this: First he coins a silly word—'tak' for instance. Then he draws various figures on the blackboard. The figures are of various shapes but some of them have a little pointed projection. He points to the figures with the projection and says: 'These are "taks".' Then pointing to the others he says: 'These are not "taks".' He would have to draw a variety of figures to indicate that it did not matter what other characteristics a figure had apart from its projection. Soon the students would be able to say themselves whether a newly drawn figure is to be called a tak or not. The impression we get from this example is that we can follow a rule by observing empirical similarities only.

There is, however, something strange in assuming that the pupils can leave the classroom and say: 'Now we know the meaning of "tak".' This is so not only because they may never see any taks outside the classroom; after all they might, on occasion, see figures that exhibit the characteristics of taks. If however they see one, what are they to do then? Should they stop and say 'tak' each time, or point it out to someone saying: 'Look here is another tak', or should they perhaps make a record of the number of taks they see each week? What is the point of the word 'tak'? The instructor gave no suggestion about this, and consequently did not teach the pupils the meaning of the word. I am not saying that he should have told his pupils something besides the rules for the proper use of the word; I am saying that he did not give the rules. What he did may have been the first step towards giving the rules but so far all that he has done is to show how to recognize the figures that are to be called 'taks' and to provide this word for them. Without the need for 'tak' in a way of life we will not start forming the notion or using the word, and the word will not acquire meaning. The need for 'tak' might arise in a factory where tak-shaped figures for some reason have to be sorted out, or in a new game where tak-shaped counters are used. Possibly the word might play a part in a larger system, of crystallography say, or meteorology, where the recognition of tak-shaped crystals or cloud-formations may help us in manipulating, controlling or predicting events.

In philosophical language it is customary to call the features of a thing that enable us to recognize it the 'criteria' for the proper use of the word that we use to refer to the thing in question. What I am saying is that these features are not the criteria for the proper use of the word: they are the features that enable us to recognize or identify the thing in question. When we see these features we don't have to use the word—except when, as we shall see, the activity of using the word is the activity of answering the question: 'Is this such and such?' On the other hand, we have to use our words at times and for purposes other than to identify a thing when we are confronted by it. Comets and revolutions do not appear or occur as often as we have occasion to talk about them. The occurrence of these phenomena is only one special opportunity to speak of them, if what we want to do is to announce their arrival or occurrence, but we do not even necessarily need to take these opportunities. The features enable us to recognize the phenomena but they enable us only to do this; they are passive, they do not tell us: 'whenever my features appear use the word x', let alone tell us what else we can or should do with a word. The features do not provide us with the rules for the use of a word and so it is misleading to think that they are the criteria for the proper use of a word. For the rules we have to look elsewhere. So in order to avoid confusion, I shall call these features not 'criteria' as they are so often called but 'recognitors'. Roughly speaking, 'recognitors' are the defining characteristics of the material elements of a thing or act or situation or any phenomenon.

Someone who would give the example of our classroom where we coined the word 'tak' as an example to show how words acquire meaning and what is necessary for a word to have meaning *does* have an activity in mind. But this activity is simply the teaching and learning of a new word. It is because we have *this* activity in mind that the example sounds convincing, but because this is a special activity the example is misleading. The pupils can perform an activity, just as the factory workers could perform the activity of sorting out tak-shaped objects, but their activity consists simply in answering the question: 'Is this a tak?' Here the rules for the proper use of the word 'tak' coincide with the recognitors of taks. Being able to answer questions like 'is this such and such?' is an important activity, but we would defeat our aim in studying the proper use of words if we unduly projected

41

this activity to the rest of mankind as if this were their main activity in using words. People use language as part of all sorts of activities. Looking for the rules for the proper use of a word or phrase is looking for the rules of those activities in which the word or phrase is employed. Even in the classroom we were given the rules for the use of the word 'tak' *for the classroom* by being given the rules for an activity: 'Say "this is a tak" whenever I draw a figure with a pointed projection'.

Language games are not word-games; they are activities of which language is a part.

2. SIMPLE EXAMPLES OF NOTIONS

a. *notions formed about the inanimate world*

Of course we do not start forming a new notion by first inventing a new word and specifying the recognitors that will enable us to answer the question 'Is this an *x*?' and *then* trying to think how we could use the word or what rules we could give for the proper use of that word. We start forming a new notion by a process which is the reverse of this.

For instance, a meteorologist may have been puzzled by a certain phenomenon and after careful observations at last connects the phenomenon with certain cloud-formations. He discovers that the phenomenon occurs five minutes after a cloud-formation which has a pointed projection. He selects these features of clouds because they enable him to perform the activity of predicting the phenomenon in question. Then he may coin the word 'tak' to refer to these cloud-formations if this is the word he wants to use to present his findings. Later, when he teaches what taks are he will be teaching at the same time the rules for predicting the phenomenon in question. People would not know what taks were if they could only recognize the cloud-formations but did not know that five minutes later a certain phenomenon will occur. We do not, then, first have words with 'neutral descriptive criteria'—or recognitors, as I would like to say—and then load them with a theory, but we select the recognitors because they are relevant to the activity in which the word will play a role. 'Tak' means more than 'being a shape with a pointed projection'. The meteorologist would rightly object to the suggestion that what 'tak' *really* meant was a certain sort of observable shape, or that the observable shape is the *fact* and the rest is added theory.

Let us suppose that during his investigations our meteorologist observed that the phenomenon occurred either five minutes after a cloud-formation with a pointed projection or five minutes after a cloud-formation when there is a hole through the cloud. In this case taks would be clouds either with a pointed projection or with a hole through them. Being a good scientist he would present his findings by saying that so far he has discovered these two different types of taks. In future he might discover other cloud-formations that look empirically different from the hitherto known taks; nevertheless they amount to the same, they are also taks. This is in line with the conclusion we came to in the first chapter when we saw that it is the formal element of a notion that enables us to decide what will or will not amount to the same thing.

Let us consider another example which clearly

illustrates that without the formal element we cannot decide what will or will not amount to a certain thing, and so cannot follow a rule in using a word. The example is quoted by Ogden and Richards on page 46 of their *Meaning of Meaning*. They quote it from what they say is a little-known book by A. Ingraham: Swain School Lectures on the *Nine Uses of Language*.

We do not often have occasion to speak, as of an indivisible whole, of the group of phenomena involved or connected in the transit of a negro over a rail-fence with a melon under his arm while the moon is just passing behind a cloud. But if this collocation of phenomena were of frequent occurrence, and if we did have occasion to speak of it often, and if its happening were likely to affect the money market, we should have some name as a 'wousin' to denote it by. People would in time be disputing whether the existence of a wousin involved necessarily a rail-fence, and whether the term could be applied when a white man was similarly related to a stone wall.

The reason why in time people would be disputing what is involved in something being a wousin is that we do not know what is the point of wousins. That this collocation of phenomena should be of frequent occurrence is not very important, as we have seen; it could occur as seldom as revolutions. More important is, as Ingraham also says, that we should have frequent occasions to speak of it. We should have occasions to speak of wousins if it were part of a ritual or if the occurrence of a wousin would be the beginning of a new year, or, as Ingraham suggests, if a wousin would be likely to affect the money market. But apart from indicating that the term might be used in our financial life he does not tell us how and for what purpose 'wousin' could actually be used.

On the view I am arguing for, we first experience an event x, say on the money-market. This event must be important enough for us to want to do something about it. We would want to promote it or avoid it or at least to understand it. Careful observers would connect the event x with the transit of a Negro over a rail-fence with a melon under his arm. Some observers would connect the relative positions of clouds and the moon to event x, others might think that the position and phase of the moon might vary as long as it was dark at the time. This disagreement would centre around the question whether the positions of the moon and the clouds are or are not connected with event x. So far there is no notion of 'wousin' in their minds; all that they are arguing about are the reasons for event x. When they have a working solution to go on, they may publish their findings, or if they are not theoreticians they may start talking about it at the stock-exchange. Thus they may coin the term 'wousin' to refer to the collocation of phenomena that constitute the reason for the occurrence of event x. The process of establishing the reasons for this event is at the same time the process of forming the rules for the proper use of 'wousin'. Furthermore, the acceptance of the rules for the proper use of 'wousin' is at the same time the acceptance of the reasons for the occurrence of event x.

A very important point to observe is that all this must be a public process. The reasons for the occurrence of the event must be publicly testable and acceptable by anyone. Otherwise, people could not use the word in the same way, the word could not become part of our language. The way, then, in which the word becomes part of our language is at the same time the way in which we publicly check that we have correctly selected certain phenomena as the reasons for the occurrence of event x.

'Wousin' then is not merely shorthand for the recognitors enumerated in Ingraham's example. It is not even shorthand for all the various different possible recognitors, that is, shorthand for a long disjunctive statement: 'either x crossing a, or y crossing b, or . . .' We have to introduce now a new word not because we want to save time but because we want to say *more* than what is stated in our disjunctive statement, we want to say that it does not matter which of these things happens so long as one of them does. This is so because they all come to, amount to the same. There was a point or reason in selecting these recognitors and from that point all the different instances of wousin are the same. This is not expressed even by stating all the possible recognitors.

b. *A notion formed about ourselves*

I would like to turn now to a third example which will bring us nearer to the formation of moral notions.

I expect the reader is familiar with those little machines which are used by bus conductors in some places for printing the tickets. Now suppose that a passenger asked for a fourpenny ticket and for some reason the conductor dialled five, thus producing the wrong ticket. He made another ticket but kept the fivepenny one as he had to account for all the tickets printed. Some time later someone else asked for a fivepenny ticket and was given the one printed earlier. So far so good, but trouble arose when the inspector boarded the bus, for since the ticket had been printed some time before the passenger got on the bus it had by now expired, and the conductor had to be called on to explain. All this was rather a nuisance as it took up the conductor's time while other passengers were getting on and off; besides, he felt that the inspector must have thought him careless and inefficient. When he came off duty he stayed to have a cup of tea at the canteen where he told the story to a group of other conductors who replied with similar stories. Some had had to do their explaining during the rush hour or to an inspector who was slow to understand. When I want to suggest that the conductors might eventually coin an expression to refer to these stories I do not of course want to say that they all suddenly decide one day: 'Well, let's call it making a misticket'. It might take several years of exchanging stories before some conductor coins this word, and perhaps even longer before it becomes general currency. Now if it is only the conductors who talk together over their cups of tea the word will become part only of their vocabulary, but if they share their discussions with the inspectors it will become part of their vocabulary as well. In the first case the word could only function as a 'nuisance-word', in the second, it could function as an 'excuse-word'. What I mean is that in the first case a conductor could not use the new word to the inspector when he wants a short-hand explanation to excuse a passenger and himself; he could only use it among the other conductors when he wants to say that this trouble has come up again. In the second case, however, he can tell the inspector: 'There is a misticket in the back', thus achieving what before the existence of this word needed a long explanation.

The difference between the two cases is not merely that the use of the word is extended to a wider group of people. The word itself will have a different function, with very important consequences. When the conductor can use this word to tell the inspector that there is a misticket in the bus he is not merely saving time by using one word instead of several: the new word is shorthand not only for a story but for a story with a point. Before the existence of this word the conductors had a point in telling the inspectors what has happened; they wanted to excuse themselves and the passenger. But the success of this excuse depended on how articulate the conductor was, how able he was to master the relevant details and leave out irrelevant ones that might only annoy the inspector; it also depended on what views the inspector had about this sort of inefficiency, on his strictness or leniency, or even perhaps on his like or dislike of the conductor. The existence of the new word changes all this. A conductor now does not need to rely on his own personal capacity to formulate and put his case well nor can the attitude of the inspector so freely influence the success of the excuse. The efficacy of the excuse is achieved by the conductors and admitted by the inspectors when the word is accepted in their common language. The rules for the proper use of the word are also rules in the way of life in which it plays a part.

At the beginning of the formation of this notion different conductors stressed various different aspects

of the occasions on which they had printed wrong
tickets, and some of these aspects eventually turned
out to be irrelevant. Only that which was common to
all their experiences was eventually incorporated into
the notion of making a misticket. This must be so if
the word is to be part of a public language. Before the
existence of the new notion, when a particular conductor related how he printed a wrong ticket, he
impressed on his audience that he had had a bother-
some experience, and his story was possibly coloured
by his subjective interpretation of the events. The
new word 'misticket' however does not refer to the
experience of an individual conductor but to that of
any conductor, and incorporates those features of the
experiences that *any* of them may have. The participation of the inspectors in the conversations
introduces not only a new group of people but an
opposite point of view and a new set of arguments for
and against the excusability of printing wrong tickets
and saving them for later passengers. As before,
irrelevances and subjective preferences have necessarily been dropped out in the course of this process.
Before the existence of this excuse-word a conductor
had to use arguments which, if they were successful,
excused only himself. The new word however, will
excuse *any* conductor, however unskilled in argument
or disliked by the inspector.

Of course, the existence of the word 'misticket' does
not settle the problem for good. Someone may sub-
sequently question whether mistickets should after
all be excused. He would not raise this question
because the arguments embodied in the notion fail
to come up to some standard or because they do not

entail that mistickets should be excused. He might raise the question because he saw a new point that could be relevant to the excusability of mistickets. Or there may be a change because of a change in the standard of efficiency or because the frequency of mistickets increases to proportions not envisaged earlier. (The cause of these might be the very existence of the new word.) These are changes connected with the formal element. The material elements could also change if the employees come to see that there are other ways in which mistickets might come about, or if the company were to introduce new machines which operate differently.

Due to the nature of the case, the number of ways in which one could make mistickets is limited, as the number of ways in which one can make tables is limited. We could readily visualize and describe the sort of thing a conductor did if we were told that he made a misticket. This does not make the term 'descriptive', not even bring it nearer to 'descriptive' terms in contrast to terms like 'mistake'. What makes a term or notion 'descriptive' or not 'descriptive' (I am making here an inverted commas use, i.e. 'what other people call "descriptive" ') is the formal element, the point of selecting and grouping together some features of the world or of our behaviour. We already have in our language words for making mistakes in more restricted situations, like 'misspelling', 'miscalculating', etc., and we could have words for a mistake in changing gears, introducing people, addressing letters, and so on. If we had a language in which there were only these more specialized words and no word corresponding to our 'mistake', it would not satisfy the requirements of our life. Since we are the sort of people that we are, the number of ways in which we can make mistakes is not limited. What the conductor did with the ticket, what the letterwriter did with the address could occur in the case of a chemist making prescriptions. We do therefore need a word which is not restricted to a limited number of situations, i.e. the word 'mistake'. Remembering that higher and lower order formal elements can constitute a hierarchy, we can say that terms like 'misspell', 'miscalculate', etc., have already organized some of the material elements of 'mistake' into their own units of material and formal elements. But not all material elements can be so further organized because there are always new ways of making mistakes. 'Mistake' is not more evaluative nor vaguer than terms like 'misspell', just as 'furniture' is not more evaluative nor vaguer than 'table'.

Not all mistakes are excused as mistickets are. In some situations with certain specifications they are, while in other cases they are not. In Chapter Four, we shall consider the differences between what I shall call 'open terms' (where further specifications are needed to enable us to make a judgment on the act) and 'complete terms' (where these further specifications have been included in the term already). 'Misticket' is complete compared with 'mistake', not simply because it tells us in what situation, in what manner and with what consequences someone made a mistake, but because these specifications came to be recognized precisely because the making of a mistake with these specifications was judged to be excusable.

We are assuming that it was eventually agreed that

conductors are excused in these cases. If, however, the outcome is different, then to say that someone made a misticket is to accuse him of inefficiency and similarly, to use it in the first person is to admit inefficiency. In this case by using the term even the most articulate conductor would admit inefficiency and the most lenient inspector would ascribe inefficiency. We further assumed that they did come to an agreement which they did not necessarily have to. If they did not come to an agreement then obviously there cannot be such a notion as misticket and the conductors cannot make mistickets, although they will continue to make mistakes in printing their tickets. On the other hand, the very existence of the word 'misticket' (and it can exist only if it is used according to rules) is a sign of the fact that they did reach an agreement and created the notion. Future generations of the employees do not need to go through the arguments again: they will grow into a form of life by learning the language of their colleagues.

But how good was the conductors' argument? How good were the reasonings that were incorporated and crystallized in the notion of 'misticket'? When the meteorologists accepted the use of the word 'tak' they also accepted the rules for predicting a certain phenomenon. The reasons for the prediction were established and agreed on when the notion of 'tak' was formed and accepted in a public language. The notion of 'wousin' had to go through a similar process. One may ask, where is the similar process in the formation of the notion of 'misticket'?

This question leads us to the consideration of one of the crucial differences between moral and other notions

The difference will turn out to be not so much a difference in the logic of their formation and structure as in their ingredients.

3. COMPARISON OF THE TWO TYPES OF NOTIONS

To begin with, I would like to claim that the excuse had to satisfy, not some abstract logical standard of proof, but the inspectors. Now this seems to be different from the formation of a notion like our 'tak'. It is true, the arguments of the meteorologist had to satisfy the other scientists but one cannot say that they had to satisfy the other scientists *tout court*. The other scientists are satisfied if they cannot find counter-examples to the meteorologist's claim, so their satisfaction depends on the presence or absence of counter-examples. This seems to be missing in the case of our misticket, until we realize that in the process of the formation of this notion it is the interests of the inspectors that correspond to the counter-examples.

A scientist needs his fellow scientists because the nature of his activity is such that it must be governed by publicly accessible criteria, but he does not need his fellows to provide the very features and aspects that he selects for his notions. In the case of our moral and social life on the other hand, it is our wants and needs, aspirations and ideals, interests, likes and dislikes that provide the very material for the formation of our notions.

With scientific notions, our interests—such as the desire to understand, predict, manipulate things or happenings—initiate and guide the selection of the recognitors, but the recognitors are of the inanimate world, or of human beings only in so far as we are also part of the inanimate world. Our interests, wants and needs enter our social and moral notions twice. As in the case of scientific notions, they initiate and guide the selection of the recognitors—though these interests are not that of wanting to predict or manipulate but of wanting to promote or avoid certain things —and secondly, the recognitors themselves are selected from our wants, needs, likes and dislikes. In forming the notion of misticket we need the employees of the bus company not only to form this notion, but to provide those relationships of wants and interests, points of view and attitudes, without which there would be nothing to form a notion of. Our sentiments do indeed enter our moral notions, but not as something extra added onto a 'pure description'. Our moral judgments do not express attitudes towards inanimate objects; if the employees were inanimate objects, not even the strongest sentiment of approbation or disapprobation towards them would help us form a moral or social notion.

Unexpectedly, the fact that our interests enter into our social and moral notions twice does not make these notions more subjective. Of course, being objective as opposed to being subjective does not mean that we talk about objects rather than about subjects. One can be subjective in talking about objects and objective in talking about subjects, i.e. about human beings and their actions. Whether we are objective depends on whether we form and use our terms according to interpersonal rules.

We have seen that the process of establishing the

recognitors and their significance must be public. This must be so not only because other people have to be able to use our terms but because not even one single person, not even the inventor of the notion, could use the new word in a consistent way without sharing its use with others. Furthermore the possibility of anyone being able to use a term in the same way is the guarantee for the fact that the recognitors and their significance have been properly selected and established.

The recognitors then, have to be publicly recognizable features of the world, and the formation of the notion must itself be a public process. But since in the case of our social and moral notions the recognitors themselves are to be found in our life, it follows that only those features of our lives can be incorporated into these notions that are shared by any of us and are recognizable by any of us, and in turn the formation of the notion must itself be done from the point of view of anyone. This if anything should make our moral notions more objective. After all, inanimate objects cannot put up any resistance if as a result of our changed interest or changed conceptual framework we select different features of the world for special attention. We on the other hand, as users of our terms, would resist such a change when the terms are about ourselves.

We saw (on p. 49) how individual variations and subjective interpretations as to what did or did not constitute a misticket had to be eliminated, and consequently that the new word did not refer to the experience of an individual conductor but to that of any conductor, and incorporated only those features of the experience that any of them might have. When the inspectors as well as the conductors together formed the notion, it acquired a new meaning and functioned in a different way. The parallel to this in the case of scientific notion would not be the introduction of a new set of scientists but the consideration of a new set of objects capable of serving as examples or counter-examples to a theory. Or, to draw another parallel which is absurd but instructive; suppose that material objects could think and feel and wanted to live together with all their needs and aspirations; in this case the consideration of a new set of objects would almost correspond to the participation of the inspectors in the discussions with the conductors, but the exact parallel would be if the objects themselves did the considering.

Another difference between our moral notions and those about the physical world which follows from this is that the latter do not affect the world which they are about. The rules for their proper use are at the same time rules for our thoughts about, or activities in, that world but they are not rules for the behaviour of the objects. The rules for the proper use of our moral notions, however, are at the same time rules for what those notions are about: they are rules for our behaviour. If Hume's oak trees had formed the notions of parricide and murder their lives would be governed by rules as well as by the 'laws of nature'.

It is not proper to say that *everybody's* wants, likes and dislikes, aspirations and ideals enter into the formation of our social and moral notions, not only because not everybody in space and time took part in their formation but because it is not a numerical universality that we need. What we should say is that only those wants, etc., that are *anybody*'s wants are incorporated in our social and moral notions, and the function and purpose of these notions in our lives must be such that anybody should be able to and should want to use them in the same way and for the same purpose. Since we form our notions from the very start from the point of view of anybody, these terms do not reflect my wants but anybody's wants. The tension between my preferences and what is good, or between what I would like to do and what I ought to do enters into our life already with our language.

I must emphasize that it is from the very start that we form our notions from the point of view of anybody. Terms used in our language are not formed by a single person who then trims them to suit others, nor are they a selection from private vocabularies made to suit, or be accepted by, others. Nor is it the case that we try to persuade others to accept our privately formed notions or that we address them to the whole world for general acceptance. I emphasize this because a large number and surprising variety of moral philosophers seem to talk about our moral life and language as if each of us spoke a private language and yet paradoxically lived in society, as if our moral notions were private notions that we try to make universal. Obvious examples of this are, for instance, the view which claims that when I say 'x is good' I express the attitude 'I like x' or 'I approve of x' and at the same time expect and try to influence others to do the same; and the view according to which a moral judgment must express a genuine want in the agent (or whatever else a first-person command addressed to oneself means) and at the same time it must be addressed to the whole world. A less obvious example is the critical as against the constructive part of Hume's moral philosophy. The fact that he regards the relationship of a son to a father as the same as that between an acorn and an oak tree shows that for him a moral agent does not live in society. The only sentiment which he considers is his own disapproval in his own breast towards what is (apparently) an inanimate world. Or again another example is the view which says that e.g. 'pain' means what I personally want to avoid, and then by means of sympathy I extend this notion of pain to others and so come to think that perhaps others would also want to avoid pain. But 'pain' does not mean 'a feeling that I personally want to avoid'. Of course, I do feel something that I want to avoid, and it is my sensation, but I can know it to be pain or recognize it as such because I learned the notion of pain. I did not form this notion myself; when I learned it and the rules for its use, I learned that anybody wants to avoid it. Furthermore, only what anyone can recognize as pain can be among the recognitors of this term.

4. FOLLOWING RULES AND GIVING REASONS

One can break the rules for the proper use of our terms with regard to both their material and formal elements. An economist may break the rules for the proper use of the term 'wousin' either by calling a group of phenomena wousin which is not recognized as such, or by not recognizing that the occurrence of wousin would cause event x on the money market. In the first case he would break the rules with regard to the material elements, in the second case with regard to the formal element. Similarly the employees of the bus company may break the rules for the use of the term 'misticket' in these two ways. A conductor may collect tickets from the box for used tickets and sell them to the passengers and then claim that they are mistickets, or an inspector may rebuke a conductor for making what is recognized to be a misticket. Again, someone may break the rules for the proper use of the term 'inadvertent' with regard to its material elements by claiming that he poisoned someone inadvertently, when in fact he carefully chose the poison that he mixed into the bowl of punch. One would break the rule for the use of this term with regard to its formal element if one claimed that someone was responsible for what he caused to happen while intending to do something else. These two ways of breaking the rules for the proper use of our terms are intrinsically connected. To see this connection is to see the unity of material and formal elements.

If our economist called anything he liked a wousin he would defeat the economists' efforts to try to predict the occurrence of event x on the money market. We would object to his calling just anything a wousin by drawing his attention to the purpose of trying to find out exactly what constitutes a wousin. And, if sometimes he said that the occurrence of wousin caused event x and sometimes that it did not, we would again object that he did not know why we selected for special recognition the group of phenomena called 'wousin'.

Thus in both cases, when the rules are broken with

regard to the material elements and when they are broken with regard to the formal elements, we appeal to the formal element. This is to be expected. Following a rule in using a word 'x' is nothing else than being able to see what are instances of x, and we cannot see what are instances of x unless we understand why they are such. We have seen that we cannot follow a rule in using a word 'x' on the basis of the empirical similarities in the material elements of the various instances of x, and this is why it is not the material but the formal element that we appeal to even when we break the rules with regard to the material elements. We have to refer to the significance of the material elements in order to claim that certain phenomena or happenings are or are not instances of x and to appeal to their significance is to appeal to the formal element. This is why it is pointless to ask how we move from the material elements to what we say a thing or act is. The fact that we can follow a rule shows that we have already made that move.

To know how to follow a rule is to know what the material element of an act amounts to. Suppose someone is trying to buy flowers, but cannot find any. If he then buys a packet of paper streamers we can say that he was trying to buy decorations, but if he comes home with a box of chocolates, we can say that he was looking for a present. If we want to find out what someone is doing who is, say, leaning against a door frame, we need to find out what he would do instead which would amount to the same thing. If he sits down, then we can say that he was resting; if he stands a beam against the frame then we can say that he was supporting it.

In the first chapter I objected to Hume's taking murder as an example of vice. There I objected on the grounds that 'murder' cannot feature in his vocabulary for it is already one of those words that do not 'stand for' a matter of fact in Hume's sense of 'fact'. Now I may add a more significant point. Had he stated his example in terms capable of featuring in his vocabulary, that is, had he stated the material elements of a vicious act, he could not have given us *another* example of *the same* vicious act. One can only follow a rule in using the word 'murder', that is, one can give other examples of murder, if one understands that the occurrence of certain material elements are reasons for claiming that they constitute murder.

Let us revive now the argument we called Argument *A* in the first chapter. Let us consider someone explaining to us why a certain object is a kettle. He will point to certain features of an object that are reasons for calling it a kettle. After having done this he cannot point to another object and say that it has the same features but it is not a kettle. This would be saying at the same time that certain features *are and are not* reasons for calling something a kettle. Thus, this argument does not only call for consistency, and does not only tie our judgments that something is such and such to the material elements: it also shows us why we have to be consistent by showing how the material elements are tied to our judgments. We have to be consistent because of the way in which we give reasons for claiming that something is such and such.

But how similar do the two objects have to be in order that we should be able to call both of them kettles? In other words, what are the features relevant to judging something to be a such and such? Obviously kettles can be made of several materials and they do not have to be round. But when it was explained to us why a certain object is a kettle, its round shape was not given as one of the reasons for calling it a kettle, and so we are not going to contradict ourselves if next time we point to a square object and call that a kettle too. Again, that it should be made of tin or steel is given only under the formal aspect of 'non-inflammable material' which allows for a certain variation of material elements. In turn, it is the formal element of our notion of a kettle which determines that a kettle should be made of non-inflammable material. We decide what are the relevant features of a kettle by referring to the point of having kettles. The features which we have to look for are those that constitute x's being the sort of thing which serves the purpose that kettles were invented to serve. So unless we can point to relevant differences between two objects, if one of them is to be called a kettle, so is the other.

By having shown how we move from the material elements to what we claim a thing or act to be, we have not bridged the 'gap' between description and evaluation. I have argued in the first chapter that these two moves should not be confused. What we have established applies both to moral and non-moral notions, to murders, lies and inadvertent acts as well as to tables and kettles. In the case of all our terms we can follow a rule in using a word 'x' only if we know what features of the world or what facts (not in Hume's sense of 'fact') are reasons for saying that something is an x. Whether we make a judgment by using a descriptive term or a moral term, i.e. whether we make a judgment like 'this is a table' or 'this is murder', the justification for our judgment lies in the presence or absence of certain relevant facts.

I am handicapped by the established terminology in expressing my views here because the terms 'descriptive' and 'evaluative' as used in contemporary philosophical literature are already committed to a theory I am trying to argue against. If there were no such commitment of the terminology I could say that we *describe* the features of the world and of our own lives for different purposes. The contrast is not, then, between descriptive and moral notions, but between description from the moral point of view as opposed to other points of view.

The way in which we move from the material element to what we claim a thing or act or situation to be is what has often been confused with the 'move from description to evaluation'. If this were a problem at all it would be present in the case of any description, whether from the moral or from any other points of view, for whenever we describe we make use of terms consisting of material and formal elements.

It is a different question to ask how we move from a description which is not a description from the moral point of view to one which is a description from the moral point of view, and this is not a problem because we would never want to make this move. The first move, the move from the material elements to what we claim something to be, is not a problem in the moral context because we always and in every context make this move; the second, the move from one type of description to another, is not a problem because we never want to make this move. The first question is like asking how we make scrambled eggs, fried eggs or omelettes out of eggs, and the second is like asking how to make scrambled eggs out of fried eggs. But just because we never make scrambled eggs out of fried eggs it does not follow that we do not make both out of eggs. Just because we never move from a description in terms of, say, civil engineering to a description in moral terms, it does not follow that they are not both based on the respective relevant facts.

If a term is formed from the legal, prudential, functional point of view, or from the point of view of one of the sciences, or from any other than the moral point of view, then in so far as these terms fulfil their respective roles they cannot be used as moral terms. *Ex hypothesi* our purposes in forming these notions are different. We cannot base a moral decision on the sorts of considerations that scientists base their decisions on. If we could, scientists would form moral rather than scientific notions. It is to be expected that only those features of the world would be incorporated into a notion that are relevant for forming that notion. So if we have a legal, scientific or functional term, then it incorporates only those features of the world that are relevant to these various points of view. The material elements grouped together under these formal elements do not provide us with reasons to come to a moral conclusion. There is nothing to prevent us, however, from using all or some of the material elements of these terms as some of the material elements of a moral term if they are relevant to the formation of a moral term. As constituents of a different notion they would be added to other material elements, for different sets of facts and different combinations of them are relevant to different notions. If we want to get from a notion which was not formed from the moral point of view to a moral notion it is only because what is incorporated in one sort of notion, or part of it, becomes relevant to the formation of another sort of notion. But then, as we have seen, there is no problem as to how we make the move, that is, there is no problem as to how to move from the material elements to what we claim a thing or act to be.

Our different sorts of notions do not cross the floor of the house: in order to get to the other side they have to go back to their constituencies and be elected for the other side. If certain material elements have been elected to serve a purpose then they serve that purpose. In order for them to serve another purpose they have to go through the same process again that enables them to serve a particular purpose, they have to be elected again.

CHAPTER THREE

COMMANDS, RULES AND REGULATIONS

WE shall take up the main theme of this study in the next chapter again. In this present chapter I would like to consider three views which provide alternatives to my general position so far. I have selected these three views not only because they are well known and influential, but because by means of them I can elucidate my position further. My aim, then, is not so much polemical as elucidatory.

First I would like to comment briefly on Aristotle's theory of the Mean in Book II, Chapter VI of his *Nicomachean Ethics*, then look at the actual text of the passage in Hume's *Treatise* that we have referred to earlier (Book III, Part I, SectionI). Thirdly, I shall analyse an important example in Mr. R. M. Hare's *The Language of Morals* (Part III, Chapter II, Section 5). The problem raised by this example will occupy most of this Chapter, giving it its title.

(1) I would like to criticize a possible interpretation of Aristotle's text without necessarily committing Aristotle to that interpretation.

Aristotle begins by saying that 'in anything continuous and divisible it is possible to take the half, or more than the half or less than the half. Now these parts may be larger, smaller and equal either in relation to the thing divided or in relation to us. The equal part may be described as a mean between too much and too little'. In the field of human actions the relevant sense of the mean is the one in relation to us. Then he turns to moral goodness within the field of human actions and claims that to find moral goodness is to find a mean in our feelings and actions.

'It is possible, for example, to experience fear, boldness, desire, anger, pity, and pleasures and pains generally, too much or too little or to the right amount. If we feel them too much or too little, we are wrong . . . The same may be said of the mean and extremes in actions. Now it is in the field of actions and feelings that goodness operates; in them we find excess, deficiency and, between them, the mean, the first two being wrong, the mean right and praised as such.' (J. A. K. Thomson's Translation).

This is sound in so far as it is a rejection of the idea that some feelings are good and others bad, and that virtue consists in having the good ones and not having the bad. Aristotle seems to be saying that our feelings and movements are raw materials out of which we can bring about virtuous or vicious dispositions and acts. This is also my position: the material elements have to constitute a significant human disposition or act in order to be judged good or bad; and since the same material elements can form parts of different acts, or the same act can be performed by the use of different material elements, the material elements by themselves are neither good nor bad.

Our Argument *A* substantiates another aspect of Aristotle's view here. Since what a thing or act is is not something extra over and above what its material elements amount to, if we want to change anything, or any act, then we have to change the material elements. If we want to turn a particular ugly object into a beautiful object we have to do something to it, and the nature of the universe is such that doing something to a thing always has a quantitative aspect in some sense.

But the idea that we can produce and/or explain these changes without reference to the respective formal elements, or the general idea that qualitative change is the result of quantitative change, is what I would reject. We do not produce beauty or virtue by quantitative change: but if by reference to these formal elements we want to produce beautiful things or perform virtuous acts then we have to make quantitative changes in the world. Furthermore, we need the formal element in order to determine in what respect and to what extent we should make these changes, we need the formal element to determine the mean. We would not even begin to look for a mean unless we aimed at certain things and we could not aim at certain things unless we had the notions of those things. Given all this we can start working out what changes we have to make in the world in order to bring about the aimed at result, and then we may call the sufficient amount of change 'the mean'.

If I complete the above quotation we can see that Aristotle's text bears this out. 'But to have these feelings at the right times on the right occasions towards the right people for the right motive and in the right way is to have them in the right measures, that is somewhere between the extremes; and this is what characterizes goodness.' This statement clearly reintroduces the need for the formal elements in order to determine what is the mean.

(2) The passage in Hume's *Treatise* I want to investigate comes after the well-known example of the acorn destroying its parent tree. When the acorn destroys its parent tree we have a relationship between two inanimate objects. Hume claims that the same relationship exists between a child and father when the child murders his father, and yet we disapprove of the latter but not of the former.

'Nor does this reasoning only prove,' says Hume, 'that morality consists not in any relations that are the objects of science; but if examined, will prove with equal certainty, that it consists not in any *matter of fact*, which can be discovered by the understanding . . . Take any action allowed to be vicious; wilful murder, for instance. Examine it in all lights, and see if you can find that matter of fact, or real existence, which you call *vice*. In whichever way you take it, you find only certain passions, motives, volitions and thoughts. There is no other matter of fact in the case. The vice entirely escapes you, as long as you consider the object. You never can find it, till you turn your reflection into your own breast, and find a sentiment of disapprobation, which arises in you, towards this action. Here is a matter of fact; but 'tis the object of feeling, not of reason.'

Let us observe what an unexpected turn this argument takes in the last sentence. If you turn your reflection to relations that are the objects of science you cannot find notions of morality. So far so good. Then you turn your *reflection* into your own breast and there you find a feeling. Observe that it is your reflection that you turned towards this feeling: the feeling which Hume claims to be a matter of fact is the new object of your reflection. From this he concludes: 'but 'tis the object of feeling, not of reason'. This conclusion is so unexpected that one could say it is a *non sequitur*. What does the 'it' refer to in the last clause? Does it refer to that matter of fact that he claims is here? But that matter of fact *was the feeling* which was the new object of his *reflection.*

I am not being fussy over a small point for this small point is largely instrumental in creating a picture that still tends to hold a large section of philosophical ethics captive. The picture is that in the world there are hard facts recognizable by reason but our reason cannot find anything which would justify us in making moral judgment or in forming a moral notion. We just have a feeling towards some facts and not towards others, the facts being the same.

Even if I were to admit that I am unfair to Hume because he was just obscure in the last sentence of my quotation, his text still cannot support his conclusion. Perhaps he wants to say that the feeling is an object of our reflection, but what we feel about, the relationship in the world, is the object of feeling. But what he says is that 'in whichever way you take it, you find only certain passions, motives, volitions and thoughts'. I assume you find these by your reflection in that relationship that you are considering. Why then is the only matter of fact difference that you find between the relationship of trees and that of humans *your own* sentiment towards the latter? When we have these material elements of 'passions, motives, volitions and thoughts', our reason forms moral notions out of them as the scientists might form scientific notions of the material elements presented by the destruction of trees.

In order to form the notion of a vicious act what we have to find is not a bit of something called *vice*. To expect this would be just as strange as to expect to find something in the relationship of the acorn and oaktree that we call *fact*. We cannot conclude that the destruction of the tree is not a fact or that it is not the object of our reason because whichever way we look at it all that we can find are certain movements, changes of colour and so on, but we do not find that matter of fact or real existence which we call fact.

Even if we keep to Hume's terminology and restrict the use of the verb 'is' to express those four relationships that he allows us to express by this verb and say that 'ought' expresses a new relationship, he is still wrong. We *did* discover those new relationships when we discovered those 'certain passions, motives, volitions and thoughts' between the child and father. The important thing to note is that these do not just colour certain hard facts but are new material elements out of which our reason forms moral notions as other aspects of the world are material elements out of which our reason forms other notions.

So I differ from Hume on at least these three points: (*a*) Not only non-moral but also the moral notions are formed by reason; what I mean by this is that the rule-following activity which is essential for the formation of any notion is the same type of rational activity in both cases.

(*b*) Although something called 'feeling' is an additional element in moral notions, it is not *my* feeling expressed towards a happening; the place of this feeling is among the raw materials which are the object of our reason—and not of feeling. If I did not also disapprove of the child's murdering his father I would not understand the notion of parricide. Beside the rational activity of disapproval—rational because it is part of the formation, understanding and use of the notion of parricide —most or all of us may have different emotional feelings about these tragedies but these are irrelevant to our investigations. They are irrelevant by reason of my third disagreement with Hume:

(*c*) The moral agent is not a lonely observer contemplating an inanimate world, not even a lonely observer contemplating other human beings. The relevant sense of feelings, etc., is the one in which these are anyone's feelings, including those of the murderer, the murdered and the observer. And of course Hume is right in finding not only feelings but also motives, volitions and thoughts in the relationships of human beings and this list can and should be extended.

(3) When I turn to Mr. Hare's example I want to re-emphasize what I said about Aristotle's example. I am going to criticize a possible interpretation of what the example could be said to exemplify without committing Mr. Hare to that interpretation. I want to say this especially in view of the qualifications made

by Mr. Hare in *Freedom and Reason* on views he allegedly expressed in *The Language of Morals* from where I take the example.

Mr. Hare would agree with Hume that no facts in the world are reasons for doing one thing rather than another. But what makes a judgment to be a moral judgment for him has nothing to do with feelings and sentiments, for reasons that contemporary philosophical psychology would support. An active principle should be provided as a major premiss to bridge the gap between the facts that are stated in the minor premiss and a moral judgment. 'A statement, however loosely it is bound to the facts, cannot answer a question of the form "What shall I do?"; only a command can do this.' (*The Language of Morals*, p. 46) 'Commands' and 'imperatives' are used interchangeably, the major premiss is an imperative in the sense that to assent to it is to assent to a command addressed to oneself as well as to others. According to pp. 168–9 this is so by definition. If one does not act on the imperative then one does not assent to it and does not use it as value judgment.

However many problems this part of the theory raises, e.g. whether the solution of the problem is made analytic or indeed what this is a solution of, they do not concern us here. The example we are concerned with tries to show the difference between imperatives and moral judgments; it tries to show that while imperatives at least implicitly always refer to individuals or particulars moral judgments are universal. To show this difference, Mr. Hare contrasts the sign 'No Smoking' with the judgment 'You ought not to smoke in this compartment'.

73

F

Suppose that I say to someone 'You ought not to smoke in this compartment', and there are children in the compartment. The person addressed is likely, if he wonders why I have said that he ought not to smoke, to look around, notice the children, and so understand the reason. But suppose that, having ascertained everything that is to be ascertained about the compartment, he then says 'All right; I'll go next door; there's another compartment there just as good; in fact it is exactly like this one, and there are children in it too'. I should think if he said this that he did not understand the function of the word 'ought'; for 'ought' always refers to some general principle; and if the next compartment is really exactly like this one, every principle that is applicable to this one must be applicable to the other. . . . On the other hand, when the Railway Executive is making the momentous decision, on which compartments to put notices saying 'No Smoking', nobody says 'Look here! You've put a notice on this compartment, so you must put one on the next to it, because it's exactly like it'. This is because 'No Smoking' does not refer to a universal principle of which this compartment is an instance. (pp. 176–7).

Mr. Hare goes on to say that if an imperative or a command is made universal, then by virtue of this fact it will become equivalent to a value-judgment. Thus if we make the imperative 'Do not ever smoke in this compartment' universal by saying: 'No one is ever to smoke in any railway compartment anywhere', he claims that 'it is not clear what could be meant by the sentence just quoted, unless it were a *moral* injunction or other value-judgment' (p. 177). Similarly, if 'Honour thy father and mother' is not addressed to the members of a chosen people but to every man, then it becomes equivalent in meaning to the value-judgment 'One ought to honour one's father and mother'.

We may remark first of all that 'Never smoke in this compartment' is claimed to be a particular, not a universal, imperative, because it refers to a single place in the British railways, while 'Honour thy father and thy mother' is a particular imperative because it is supposedly addressed to a single group of people. This observation may help us later on to distinguish to some extent between rules and regulations made by competent authorities over the *area* of their jurisdiction, and commands and orders given by competent authorities to people under their jurisdiction. In the first case one can extend the area over which the rule is applicable; in the second one can extend the number or class of people to whom the command is addressed. But in the first case even if the area is restricted the rule is applicable to everyone, and in the second even if the command is restricted to a group of people no restriction of place is implied. Thus, nobody can say that a 'No Smoking' sign on a particular compartment is not addressed to him, and especially one cannot say that it is not addressed to everyone because the sign is not put on every compartment.

As a matter of fact Mr. Hare is not contrasting the logical force of the sign 'No Smoking' with the injunction 'Do not smoke in the presence of a child', but with the putting up of the *physical object*, the 'No Smoking' sign itself. What the supposed objector objects to is that the sign itself is not put on every compartment. We shall see presently that this is not a deficiency in universality but is the very nature of regulations: we do not protest to the manager of a department store if he puts an 'In' sign over one door and an 'Out' sign over the other, although the two doors look exactly alike.

Both the sign and the child can be reasons for not smoking, though as we shall see, quite different sorts of reasons. Once we have accepted the presence of a child (or of a sign) as a reason for not smoking—as *ex hypothesi* it happened in Mr. Hare's example—then one cannot at the same time say that the presence of a child is *not* a reason for not smoking, as one would do if one behaved like the person in the example. It is for this reason, and not because of some reference to a universal principle, that one should not smoke in the next compartment either if there is a child in it too. The same applies to the 'No Smoking' sign if one regards it as a reason for not smoking. One cannot say: 'All right I shall go next door, there is a "No Smoking" sign there too, and I shall smoke there'.

In saying this I am not intending to eliminate the differences between moral injunctions, judgments and advice on the one hand, and rules, regulations, commands and orders on the other. But before we can draw these distinctions we have to eliminate a confusion due to a misleading comparison, that is, the comparison of the logical force of a statement like 'You ought not to smoke where there is a child in a compartment', to the putting up of a physical object, the 'No Smoking' sign, on various compartments. (To see what is compared to what in the example one should reverse the comparison and we then get the absurd objection addressed to the mother: 'Look here! You brought a child to this compartment so you should bring a child to the one next door because it is exactly like this one.')

Now if we observe what different sort of reasons the

child and the sign are for not smoking then the contrast intended in the example will be reversed. The sign, unlike the child, is a reason for not smoking only if we refer to a general principle like 'No one is to smoke in a compartment where there is a sign like this put up by a competent authority'. But the sign by itself is not, as the presence of a child is, a reason for not smoking. Continental railways may illustrate my point better. On some continental railways a simple triangular sign without words is put on non-smoking compartments. A triangular sign by itself, without reference to a rule or regulation, is not a reason for doing anything. This type of example could be used as an illustration by someone who would like to claim that practical reasoning conforms to a deductive argument where the minor premiss simply states a fact from which no obligation can follow. If we stated in a minor premiss that there is a triangular sign on a window we would not be given any reasons for doing anything. For this sort of minor premisses commands, rules and regulations are obvious major premisses if as a conclusion we would like an injunction for doing or not doing something. This however does not help us in the analysis of moral judgments. The presence of a child is not like the presence of a triangle which by itself does not provide us with a reason for doing or not doing something. If we read the example carefully, we see that the person addressed looked round, noticed the child and so understood the reason. We remarked already that the reason why he then could not say that he will smoke in the next compartment where there is also a child is not because there is a further general principle beyond what he already understood, but because if he accepted the reason he could not at the same time reject it.

Next, let us see why the sign is not put on every compartment that looks the same. The sign is part of the rules and regulations of the railways. The reason for having regulations is that some people want to do one thing and others another and so their behaviour has to be regulated. A conscientious Railway Authority may conduct a survey on the smoking habits of people before they put up their signs. If they discover that only thirty per cent of their passengers are non-smokers then they will put 'No smoking' signs only on thirty per cent of their compartments. If they discover that smokers like to sit in carriages near the engine then they will put the signs on the rear carriages. But the reason for putting up the signs does not depend on certain features of the compartment and this is why we cannot protest to the Railway Executive: 'Look here! You've put a notice on this compartment, so you must put one on the next to it, because it is exactly like it.' As we noted, we do not put an 'In' sign over all doors that look exactly alike. (There can be a 'No Smoking' sign on a compartment because of certain features of the compartment, e.g. when it is made of inflammable material, but then the sign is not a regulation but a warning. In this case it would be inconsistent not to put a sign on all compartments that are alike in this respect. Warnings need to be given if we could not by ourselves detect the reason for doing something; if we could detect it, this case would be similar to the presence of the child: by looking around we would notice the inflammable material and so understand the reason for not smoking, and

78

we would not smoke in the next compartment either if it was also made of the same material.)

It is perfectly conceivable that no one would be allowed to smoke on any railway compartment anywhere. This would not turn the regulation into a proper universal and thereby into a moral judgment; it would turn the regulation into a rule. It would then be sufficient to put a sign to this effect at a suitable place on the station.

I quoted Mr. Hare as saying that only a command can be an answer to a question of a form 'What shall I do?' so we should glance equally briefly at some aspects of commands. When the Railway Authorities put up a 'No Smoking' sign they are not issuing a command. They may give orders to their employees but they have no authority over the passengers to give them orders, let alone commands. They have authority over certain *places* where they can make rules and regulations. As rules and regulations are restricted to or are applicable to certain places, commands are restricted to groups of people over whom the authority extends. While reference to a commanding authority is essential for the analysis of commands, here I would like to touch on another aspect of the logic of commands, an aspect similar to what we noticed about regulations.

We noticed that although there are reasons for making regulations, these reasons are not necessarily given in the situation where the regulation is made. Thus, for instance, we do not find the reason for the presence of the 'No Smoking' sign in the compartment where it is placed. Similarly, although there are reasons for issuing commands, they are not necessarily in the situation about which the command is made. An officer in the army could command one morning 'Use the starting handle' and next morning command 'Run around the block'. The reason for the command was to make the recruits fit or to make them obedient, so none of them could protest next morning that although the cars were in the same condition and the temperature was the same yet they were not commanded to use the starting handle again. This is unlike the case when I give *advice* on how to start a car which is in a certain condition in a certain temperature. If the temperature and the condition of the engine are the reasons for my advice then if again the same reasons are present I have to give the same advice. This difference between the command 'Use the starting handle!' and the advice 'Use the starting handle' is not due to the alleged fact that the one is not while the other is a universal imperative. The discrepancy in the consistency in following a rule is due to the different reasons for saying that one should use the starting handle.

It would be instructive to consider a case where a command resembles a piece of advice in that it is given on the basis of the relevant facts of the situation. On the battlefield the officer might command 'Move forward' because of certain facts in the situation. If he thinks his reasons are correct, then next time when the same facts are present he will give the same command. The soldier who moves forward might not know the reasons, either because he is inexperienced or because he does not know all the facts about the situation. (We may compare this to the case when the 'No Smoking' sign was a warning.) Since he is ignorant of the facts and their significance, only a command can answer his question 'What shall I do?' This is especially so in a military context where sometimes one should *not* do something unless commanded to do it. The commanding officer however has reasons for commanding 'Move forward'. If his reasons for giving the command were in the situation, then if another situation is the same in the relevant respects he will give the same command again. In fact this is what is happening even in the training-camp when his reasons for giving the command is to make the recruits fit. If the same reason is present he will give appropriate commands. But since there are many ways of making recruits fit he can command first one thing and next time another thing. If something else can achieve the same purpose that moving forward on the battlefield achieves then on the battlefield the officer can vary his commands too.

Again, just as we noted in the case of regulations, we can note in the case of commands that they provide some of the few examples where practical reasoning has a deductive form. However much the recruits in the training ground would investigate the facts they would find no reason either for using the starting handle or for running around the block. So in cases like this, beside stating a fact like 'this is a starting handle', we would need a command as a major premiss if we want to have the injunction 'use this' as a conclusion. But this is not the pattern of moral reasoning. When we told someone to use the starting handle as a piece of *advice* we did so because of certain facts, because of the condition of the engine and the temperature. That these facts were the reasons for doing something is shown by considering that it would be inconsistent not to give the same advice again if the same facts are present again. Moral judgments are like pieces of advice in that they are made on the basis of the relevant facts of the situation. The reasons for *doing* what a piece of advice or a moral judgment tell us to do are the same relevant facts of the situation and not some logical features of the speech act, that is, not that the advice or the moral judgment is an imperative or command. We need to give advice or make a moral judgment if the person addressed does not know the relevant facts and/or their significance. Otherwise the justification for giving advice and for doing what is advised is the same. It is not the case then that we need a reference to a command or to an imperative in explaining why we do something. Far from commands being the reason for even doing anything, issuing commands is just one of the things that we do. The recruit in the army was doing something for no other reason than that he was commanded to do it, but the officer did not give the command for no other reason than that he in turn was commanded to do so. If we consider that even to make a descriptive statement is to do something, we realize the fundamental inadequacy of explaining why we do something in terms of commands and imperatives.

We do not get a moral judgement or something equivalent to a moral judgment by making commands, rules or regulations universal. We have seen that commands are or can be restricted with regard to the people addressed while rules and regulations are or can be restricted with regard to the places to which they apply. If they are lumped together under the umbrella term 'imperatives', following grammar book divisions, then a certain ambiguity results as to what we should do in order to make imperatives universal. We might think of extending the range of places to which rules and regulations apply, as we did when we eliminated the reference to British Railways; or we might think of extending the number or class of people addressed, as we did when we addressed 'Honour thy mother and thy father' to all men. Whichever way we take universality it is not the distinguishing mark of moral judgments. When a dictator aspires to address his commands to all men over the whole world, he is not aspiring to turn his commands into moral judgments.

With moral judgements the question of universality does not arise. They are not commands that can be addressed to some or all people, they are claims about situations in which something should or should not be done. The validity of these claims can be impugned only by reference to the relevant facts of the situation. So unless a person by being in the situation makes a relevant difference to the situation, the claim applies to him. They are not addressed to everybody, they apply to anybody. If the same situation is present again we have to make the same judgment. This is not universality but rationality. In the next chapter we shall see that the importance of moral notions is that they group together for us some of the important and most often recurring configurations of morally relevant facts.

But first I want to make three further brief observations on the differences and connections between commands, rules, regulations and moral judgments, observations which open up further problems rather than solve them.

(1) It seems that rules and regulations are formulated in such a manner as to enable people to follow them on the basis of empirical similarities, e.g. 'do or do not do something wherever there is such and such a sign'. This must be so partly for a logical reason: if people do not know why they should or should not do something then only empirical similarities could enable them to follow a rule. It must also be so for practical considerations. Rules and regulations have to be enforced, punishments or penalties may be attached to breaking or breaching them, insurance claims may be connected with them. It is easier to enforce and observe rules and regulations if they are formulated in terms of empirical similarities. This may create a certain discrepancy between some of our rules and regulations and our moral judgments. Someone may refrain from smoking in an empty 'No Smoking' compartment and smoke where the regulation allowed him though there are several children present.

(2) While in our daily life we have to be aware of the possible discrepancies between the content of some rules and regulations and some moral judgments, my second point is that rules and regulations, however neutral they may be from the moral point of view, can take on a moral significance. Rules and regulations can create expectations that we want to rely on and sometimes are entitled to rely on. This may give to the observance of rules and regulations a moral significance even though they are about morally neutral or even trivial matters. In order that expectations would not be frustrated, everybody's co-operation is needed. I think that some of the utilitarian theories

draw our attention to the moral significance of this type of universality, but this type of universality is different from the ones we have been considering. The area of our life where this problem is significant is restricted to cases where everybody's co-operation is necessary for the success of an operation, e.g. to cases like the observance of water restrictions, observance of the rule of the road or clean air regulations. Although one cannot see anything wrong in watering one's garden, the appeal 'what would happen if everybody did the same' is legitimate and significant because the operation in question, water restriction, is a communal, corporate activity. But if we were to extend this type of argument to cover the whole field of moral life absurdities would follow. It is true that if everyone left his wife disaster would follow, but this is not the reason why I should not leave my wife. Leaving one's wife is not like watering the garden in that one cannot see anything wrong with it without the appeal 'what would happen if everybody did the same'.

G. E. Moore argued that murder is wrong because if murder were a general practice it would create insecurity, and 'the feeling of insecurity, thus caused, would absorb much time, which might be spent to better purpose, is perhaps conclusive against it', i.e. against committing murder. (*Principia Ethica*, pp. 156–7.) Again this may be true, but this is not the reason for not murdering someone.

(3) My third point not only concerns the logic of commands but is crucial for the correct handling of the connections between what is usually called 'description' and 'evaluative judgments'.

When I issue a command my speech act must include or else refer to a description of what I command you to do. There may of course be conventions simplifying our linguistic conventions, as for instance when soldiers have to stop at the sound of a whistle, but these special cases can be dealt with without invalidating the obvious point I am making. Similarly, when I make a prediction of a future event I must describe in my prediction what future event I am predicting, and when I give you advice or tell you what you ought to do, naturally I must state what you ought to do. If we wish, we can separate out this part of the speech act and write it down in a sentence which, according to grammarians' classification, would be in the indicative mood. Some philosophers then might go on to say that this is the 'descriptive content' or 'descriptive element' of imperatives, commands and moral judgments. There must be then another element in these speech acts that makes them commands, predictions or something else. This is not only harmless but has its intrinsic value when our object is to work out a system of formal logic for sentences that are not in the indicative mood. We can make a fundamental mistake however, if we assume that in looking for a connection between statements of fact on the one hand, and commands, predictions and moral judgments on the other, we should be looking for a connection between *this* 'descriptive content' and what differentiates these various speech acts into commands, predictions, etc. For the 'descriptive content' of these various speech acts is not the relevant description we are interested in in this context.

For instance, if I command you to shut the door, or

advise you to do so, or for some reason say that you ought to shut the door, or predict that this is what you are going to do, we find a common descriptive element in all these speech acts: 'your shutting the door soon'. We may call this the 'what' of these speech acts, since it tells us what it is that we should or shall do. The 'what' in our examples so far does not tell us *why* we should do what we are told to do. When we are interested in the connection between 'description' and 'evaluation', we are interested precisely in this question, namely whether we can give reasons for saying that you must or ought to do something by reference to some facts that can be stated in 'descriptive statements'. Since as we have seen in our examples, the 'what'—the supposed 'descriptive element'—does not tell us why we should do what we should do we may come to the wrong conclusion that no description can be given as the reason for doing something. But the 'descriptive element' does not give us the reason why we should do what we are told to do—not because it is a 'descriptive element', but because it is not the relevant description we are interested in. The 'what' tells us only what we should do, and the set of facts we should be interested in is the set that gives us the reasons for doing what we are told to do. Examples of this other set of facts could be in this case that there is a draught and I have a cold or that there is noise and we want to discuss something, or in the case of a moral judgment, the fact that there is a tetanus patient in a hospital room who should be protected from noise. But in none of these cases does the 'what' tell us why we should do or say something, not even in the case of predictions, unless we are clairvoyant.

This confusion of the relevant facts with the 'descriptive content' of certain statements can be illustrated by a more popular example. We are often told that we cannot move from the statement 'the cat is on the mat' to 'the cat ought to be on the mat'. Of course we cannot. But why we cannot move from the one to the other is not because one is a 'descriptive statement' and the other is an 'ought judgment', but because the fact that the cat is on the mat is not a reason for saying that the cat ought to be on the mat. If there are reasons for saying that the cat ought to be on the mat they are a different set of facts.

What I have been saying applies primarily to commands and only to some extent to moral judgments. To see this we have to recall that the reason for what is commanded is not necessarily in the situation in which or about which the command is made, while on the other hand, moral judgments state what in certain situations should or should not be done. If a speech act states merely what some people should do, then we do not find the reason for doing it in the speech act. But if a speech act states what in certain situations should be done then the speech act may include the reason for doing what we are told to do. At the same time the more we know of the reasons the greater choice we have in the ways of implementing what should be done, that is, we have a greater choice as to *what* we should do. If we assume that the 'what' is the only descriptive content to think about we might get the impression that the descriptive content of such speech acts is left vague.

For instance, the soldiers were simply commanded what to do—theirs not to reason why. The descriptive content of the command—moving forward or using the starting handle—is not the reason for doing what they were told to do. Not even in the case of advice or of moral judgments is it necessarily the case that by being told what to do we are also told why we should do it, though this could happen, and when we use a *moral notion* in our moral judgment it *does* happen that we are given the reason. When we use moral notions, we express why something should be done as well as what should be done, because, as we shall see in the next chapter, moral notions group together in one term the morally relevant facts of certain situations.

When I say 'Do not smoke', I tell you what not to do without saying why not to. The reason may be because the compartment is small and there is a child in it. So when I say 'Do not smoke in a small compartment in the presence of a child' I also say why you should not do what I tell you not to do. If we had in our language one term 'x' for smoking in a small compartment in the presence of a child then 'x' would be a moral term and I could say 'x is wrong'.

When we had a moral reason for saying 'Shut the door', the reason for shutting the door was that a tetanus patient had to be protected from noise. Let us suppose that in hospital and medical circles the term 'tetprotect' is used to state that since noise is a mortal danger to tetanus patients appropriate measures should be taken when such a patient is in hospital. If the doctor uses this term to state what the nurse should do, then if the nurse understood the term she understood not only the 'what' but also why the request was made. We can also see a familiar feature of

89

our moral notions in this example. 'Tetprotect' can be exemplified by putting sawdust on the road outside, by wearing soft shoes or by shutting the door. Not only should the nurse understand why she should do something if the doctor tells her to enforce or bring about tetprotection, unless she knew the reason she would not quite know *what* to do and she would not know that all these different activities are examples of the same thing. Without such a term the doctor would have to tell the nurse simply *what* to do.

For a proper analysis of this one would also have to go into the vast problem of the differences between the reasons for what we say, the reasons for saying it at all and the reasons for the manner in which we say it. The reason why the door ought to be shut is different from the reason why I have to say at all that it ought to be shut. There are further special reasons why sometimes it has to be commanded, e.g. when the nurse just would not do it otherwise. But in the case of moral judgments at least, the reason for what I say, namely that the door ought to be shut, and the reason for shutting it are the same: the relevant facts of the situation. It is important to realize this, especially in contrast to theories that would separate, *both* (1) the justification of an 'ought judgment' *and* (2) the reason for doing something, from the facts of the situations, and instead of preserving the relation of each of these to the facts, connect them to each other. In the case of these theories the reason why I do something is explained by reference to some feature of a speech act, i.e. that it is a command addressed to me.

We had to go through these arguments not only to show that the logic of commands is not the model for

90

the analysis of moral judgments, but because by doing so we are able to indicate the role that moral notions play in our language. After clearing away a few more difficulties we shall address ourselves in the next chapter more directly to the function of moral notions in our language.

CHAPTER FOUR

MORAL NOTIONS AND
MORAL JUDGMENTS

1. MEN OF PRINCIPLES AND MORAL PRINCIPLES

IN this Chapter we shall investigate the role moral notions play in our moral judgments. By moral judgments I mean judgments like 'lying is wrong', 'promises ought to be kept' and also judgments like 'it is you who should stay with your mother and your brother should join the resistance movement'. While moral notions play a role in the first two judgments, the third does not incorporate a moral notion.

Before we can embark on this investigation we have to clear away another problem. We have to investigate first the use of the term 'moral principle' because it could be argued that the first two of my examples were examples of moral principles and only the third is an example of a moral judgment. It could further be argued that the third example is a particular moral judgment applying general moral principles to a particular situation, or, as someone with an existentialist persuasion might say, it is a moral judgment simply.

In the next section of this Chapter we shall find that there is some justification for making this distinction. In one particular sense of 'principle' we can say that judgments like 'lying is wrong' provide us with a principle. But this particular sense of the term will not be sufficient to separate my three examples from the point of view of their logic. Rather, I shall be justified in assimilating them in view of the great difference in the logic of this particular sense of 'principle' and other uses of this term. I am not here concerned with terminology in the sense of wanting to correct or change everyday usage, but I want to distinguish between different uses of a term for the sake of what I think to be greater clarity in philosophical analysis.

The term 'principle' has a long and rich history from the translation of Aristotle's term 'arche' to the present day. The history of science and mathematics as well as the history of our moral life have affected its life and meaning. Because of its rich history we have to be careful when we use this term in moral philosophy. The use of a single umbrella term to cover a wide variety of judgments and other performances can be convenient if it is a neutral technical term which, however, the term 'moral principle' is not. Its use could commit us to a particular view of our moral life and language.

'Being a principle' is not a feature of statements or judgments. It is people—and only some people—who make and have principles or live according to principles. Moreover, the term 'principle' is used outside our moral life, in science, for instance, in such a way that to understand what being a principle is we have to understand the place of certain propositions in a system. The association of this term with scientific systems and reasonings should make us careful in our philosophical analysis when we use the term 'moral principle'.

We can decide to make a principle about almost anything. We can decide to get up every morning at the crack of dawn, or not to eat tomatoes, or never to leave kerosene heaters alight in an empty house, on principle.

Let us consider how we would question the wisdom of an act when it is and when it is not done on principle. If someone gets up with the sun every morning because he thinks it makes him healthy, or if someone refuses to eat tomatoes because he thinks they increase the blood pressure, then these acts are not done on principle. To question their wisdom we can produce medical evidence on the subject and dispute the justifications offered for them. If, however, someone says that he does these things on principle the whole procedure of challenging the wisdom of his acts will change. Not that we cannot question or challenge them, only we have to adopt a different approach. People do have reasons for adopting certain principles, but these are not based on the actual situations in which the acts are performed. Whenever reference is made to a principle the argument is shifted away from the merits or demerits of the action in question to a different field.

A person may think that tomatoes are both delicious and health-giving, but since he disapproves of the activities of the Tomato Marketing Board, he refrains from buying and eating tomatoes on principle. It would be out of place to tell him about the merits of eating tomatoes because he knows that tomatoes are good and even likes them. The only point on which we can argue with him is his disapproval of the Marketing Board, but then we would shift the argument from the merits of eating tomatoes to the merits of the Marketing Board.

There are many patterns of adopting and behaving according to principles. One case could be that the person does not mind if his acts do not affect the Marketing Board: his not eating tomatoes is the expression of the genuineness and sincerity of his disapproval. Cases like this indicate why we sometimes respect people who act on principles even when we disagree with them, and in these cases perhaps the only appropriate praise is for their sincerity. I want to outline however two different patterns of adopting and behaving according to principles, two patterns that exhibit some similarities to patterns of behaviour we have considered in the previous chapter in connection with commands, rules and regulations.

The commanding authority, which is so important in explaining why we obey commands, is absent in the case of principles. But we have seen that there are other reasons for doing things beside being commanded to do them; there are reasons for issuing commands and also reasons for making things matters of principle. So let us consider, as against the above case, a more likely one, when the person who disapproves of the Marketing Board would like to effect changes in the Board. If his acts are to have any significance they must take on the pattern conforming to the pattern of water restrictions and clean air regulations in so far as his act must be part of a corporate act. He must make the principle universal: 'nobody should eat tomatoes'.

What is happening in this case is that the person's act, what he is doing, is not simply eating or not eating tomatoes, but is aimed at changing the policy of the Board. If we apply the test I mentioned on page 60 and ask, if for some reason he cannot avoid eating tomatoes, what alternatives are open to him that would amount to the same act, then in his case the alternatives would not be the taking of drugs to counteract the supposed ill effects of tomatoes or the pouring of seasonings on them to counteract their taste. These would be the alternatives if his acts were simply the not eating of tomatoes and the reasons for them lay in the merits of eating or not eating them. In our present case, as alternatives he might organize pickets outside the Board Office, write letters to the papers or lobby parliamentarians. Or, to apply a further test, if the Carrot Marketing Board adopted the same policy then it would be carrots that he would stop eating. What he is concerned about is not the eating of tomatoes in so far as they are tomatoes but in so far as eating them is the material element of a different act, the act of changing reprehensible policies. We could put it this way: it is not a matter of eating tomatoes but a different matter, a matter of principle. The pattern of the act is the same as in the case of the slogan 'Support local goods'. The very nature of the act is such that it must be corporate and this is why we need universality. How many people should co-operate in the act depends on the nature of the act. Two people are sufficient for performing the act of quarrelling or singing a duet, but more are needed for an orchestral performance. Still more people are needed if the act is aimed at supporting local goods.

It is very important to see what function is played by universalizing in connection with these acts. It is not the case that we want everybody—or most people—to perform the same act, but that we need the co-operation of all or at least most people, in order to perform an act at all. When I want another person to sing with me what I want is not more than one person to sing solos but another person to sing in order to sing a duet. If my reasons for not eating tomatoes were their supposed detrimental effect on health then equally of course I would try to persuade others not to eat this harmful vegetable, but this is not a case of refraining from eating them on principle.

As the pattern of reasoning behind obeying commands or following rules and regulations lends itself to being represented in a deductive argument, so the pattern of reasoning behind acting on principle could give the same impression. We do not know why we should buy something which is a local commodity unless we are given a major premiss 'Buy local goods'; we cannot see anything wrong with eating tomatoes unless we are asked not to eat them on principle. The various local goods or the tomatoes are given in a 'descriptive' minor premiss and reasons for doing anything about them cannot be derived from these minor premisses. It is very often the case that we would not buy some of the local goods unless we were doing it on principle. But what we are asked to do when we are asked to do these things on principle is not to take note of a major premiss from which certain obligations may follow but to regard our act as amounting to a different act: we are asked to regard the tomatoes not as food but as the commodity of a certain Marketing Board, and to regard a cake-mixer not as an instrument that mixes the ingredients more or less efficiently but as a product of someone of your own community. Nor do we deduce our principle from a still higher principle: we have reasons for disapproving of the Marketing Board or for supporting local manufacturers. An appeal to a principle functions like a lever that shifts the reason for one's acts to a different ground. To some extent the pattern of behaviour in buying local goods could be compared to the behaviour of a farmer who is sorting apples according to official standards. (The difference is that we are reintroducing a competent authority who sets up the standards.) The farmer does not look at the properties of the apple and ask: 'Are these good reasons for claiming this apple to be Super Grade?' He looks at the properties of his apples simply to recognize whether they satisfy the official standards or not. He does not make value-judgments, he does not evaluate apples: he is sorting them. But in sorting his apples he does not regard the official standard as major premises and the description of the properties of the apples as minor premises. He appeals to a standard. There are reasons for setting up these standards and when he appeals to them he is shifting the reasons for classing certain apples as Grade A from the merits of his particular apples to those reasons that were adduced for setting up the standards. Such standards are called for where disputes may arise which for some reason should be avoided, or where uniformity is desirable.

Reference to a principle does not make an act a moral act. Whether the act is moral or not cuts across the distinction between doing something on principle or not on principle: it depends on the sort of reason we have for doing something either way. If tomatoes caused cancer then not eating them could be a moral matter, though it is not on principle that we stop eating them. On the other hand if we disapprove of the Marketing Board because we think that marketing should not be organized by a group of bureaucrats, then although we stop eating tomatoes on principle our act will not be a moral matter. The two cases coincide, if, for instance, the Board knowing the ill effects of tomatoes, goes on advertising them.

Let us turn now to another pattern of adopting and behaving according to principles. There are reasons for not leaving a kerosene heater alight in an empty house. Whenever these reasons are present we should turn the heater off. But sometimes these reasons may not be present, as when there is no possibility of a draught, there are fire guards around the heater and so on. According to our analysis of the rationality of human acts, one could leave the heaters on when the reasons for putting them out are not present. But can we be sure? 'I know there are no reasons for putting it out now', someone could say, 'but I put the heater out on principle.' This is similar to the case when someone knew all the reasons for eating tomatoes and even liked them and yet refused to eat them on principle. But now the reference to a principle does not shift the reasons so far away from the actual reasons for not leaving heaters on in empty houses. One adopts a principle now because one does not want to rely on the actual reasons for putting the heater out each time. We might not be able to ascertain all the facts, some unknown contingency could arise, we might be careless or complacent, so it is better to lay down a firm rule and on principle never leave heaters on in an empty house.

One could argue that here again we are performing a different act if we do what we do on principle. As in the previous case the movements of consuming the vegetable came under the formal element of disapproval of certain policies and not under the formal element of eating, so now the movements of putting out the flames come under the formal element of cautiousness and not under that of fire prevention, and this is what makes a difference to the following of rules. For our present purposes we do not need to go into this problem. It is enough for us to observe that in this case rule-following has been simplified by following empirical similarities. This is more like the case of not smoking wherever there is a 'No Smoking' sign. Such simplifications are important where we cannot rely on our own judgments, where the nature of the case is such that unforeseen contingencies could arise or where we are prone to carelessness. Mothers are wise always to close safety pins or always to put cold water into the bath before the hot, on principle. A doctor may advise someone whom he cannot continually visit to take a certain pill as soon as the slightest signs of a symptom appear. The doctor would know that half of the time the pill would not be necessary but he has to simplify the rules for someone who does not know the reasons for taking the pill. Here we have again a pattern of behaviour such that the reasoning behind it can be exemplified in a deductive argument. *When* we should do something can be stated in a 'descriptive' minor premiss, and *ex hypothesi* the reasons for doing something are not in this description. We do something on these occasions by reference to a principle. If one's life is conducted according to principles of this type, the relevant facts of the situation are not given as reasons for one's acts or for one's decisions. The relevant facts of the situation serve only to enable us to recognize that here is a case that falls under a principle.

If we took this pattern of behaviour as the typical example of following a rule then our Argument A (of Chapter One, p. 28) could be made to look quite different. In this case the reason why one cannot say that in situation X one should do something but in situation Y which is like X in all relevant aspects one should not do it, is because if we were to say this we could not teach our principles to others and they would not know how to recognize what falls under our principle. I tried to show earlier that Argument A illustrates the behaviour of people who have reasons for doing something. But this argument can be made to look like a guide for those who do not know the reasons for doing something.

As I said, there are special situations and cases where acting on principles of this type is called for. Our literature is full of examples of people who extend this to cases and situations where such a pattern of behaviour is not called for. There are occasions for being kind, visiting friends in hospitals and making polite conversation. One should hope that we know when these occasions arise and when they do not, and so we do not need to do these things on principle.

The sense of universality in this type of principle is different from the sense of universality involved in our previous type. There it was a question of all or most people doing something, now it is a question of always doing something or doing something in all cases of such and such. In this respect the first type exhibits similarities to commands, the second to rules and regulations. In connection with the second type of principle we also find a parallel to the possible discrepancy we found between following some of our rules and regulations on the one hand and our moral judgments on the other.

We have considered briefly two patterns of behaving according to principles. There are many other patterns each exhibiting special characteristics and logic. Different reasons, different situations and circumstances call for the adoption of principles in different restricted areas of our lives. Some are connected with virtues, when living according to principles or rules is regarded as an exercise in obedience or self discipline, while on the other end of this scale we might find cases of moral immaturity or fear of responsibility. A nice example of yet another use of 'principle' is provided by one of the first quotations under the relevant sense of 'Principle' in the *Oxford English Dictionary* (No. 7 out of 11 senses). It comes from Cromwell: 'If I were to choose any servant . . . I would choose a godly man that hath principles . . . Because I know where to *have* a man that hath principles.' My primary aim in this excursion was to show that being a principle is not a property of certain judgments; it is people who regard certain things as matters of principle, who adopt certain principles or behave according to principles. Consequently the term 'moral principle' should be used with caution as a term in philosophical analysis.

I considered two patterns of behaving according to principles out of the many because I thought that perhaps these two may have had some influence on some of the contemporary analyses of our moral language and reasoning.

At the beginning of this chapter I said that perhaps I could not object to anyone giving as an example of moral principles 'lying is wrong'. I am not concerned about terminology but I am concerned about the difference between the *judgment* 'lying is wrong' and somebody's not lying *on principle*. One could of course make a principle about lying and could decide never to tell a lie under any circumstances, not even in order to save a man's life, but this is different from making the judgment that lying is wrong. If we ever justify our not doing something by reference to such a judgment as 'lying is wrong' we are not appealing to a principle. (In fact, for a reason that we shall see on page 124, namely that the word 'wrong' functions here only as a reminder, it is enough to say 'but this is a lie'.)

2. SITUATIONS AND MORAL NOTIONS

Until we can see why I want to call judgments like 'lying is wrong' as well as judgments like 'it is you who should stay with your mother and your brother should join the resistance movement' moral judgments, we shall temporarily refer to the first type of judgment as 'moral principles' in inverted commas. There seems to be a difference between the two types of judgments that may invite one to call the first 'moral principles', and while we discuss this difference we might as well use this inverted commas device.

There are few such 'moral principles', at least fewer than one might expect. Their form is 'X is right (or wrong)' or 'X ought (or ought not) to be done' and their number is restricted by the number of terms we can substitute for 'X'. Of course we can judge an unlimited number of actions right or wrong if we state or indicate the relevant facts of the situations in which they are performed. Without that the act may or may not be right. What we mean by saying that the act may or may not be right is that its rightness or wrongness depends on the relevant facts of the situation in which they are performed. We may recall here our brief reference to Aristotle's theory of the mean in the previous chapter. Our feelings and acts can be right or wrong; to have them or perform them 'at the right times on the right occasions towards the right people for the right motive and in the right way . . . is what characterizes goodness'. But if for 'X' in the above forms we substitute not only a verb or verbal noun specifying an act but also terms specifying some of the relevant facts of the situation in which the act is performed then our judgment will not look like a 'moral principle' but more like my example 'it is you who should stay with your mother. . . .' (I referred to the resistance movement to indicate at least the type of situation in which the choice is made and the references to 'you' and 'brother' far from making the judgment applicable only to two particular individuals at least indicates that there must be some extra facts in the situation which are reasons for *this* choice.)

If someone were to ask whether it is right or wrong to utter certain sounds our immediate reaction would be to say 'it depends'. It depends on what human act the uttering of sounds amounts to and for what reason and in what situation that act is performed. Uttering sounds 'in itself' is neither right nor wrong. What we mean by 'in itself' is that without that additional information we are not able to judge it right or wrong. Suppose someone were to begin to give the additional information by putting the question this way: 'Is it right or wrong to utter certain sounds when the sounds are uttered according to certain rules and conventions that exist in a society . . . ?' In fact we have one word for uttering sounds with these qualifications, we do not need to state the movement and then add all these qualifications; we have the verb 'saying (something)'. All this extra information is still not enough, we should still say 'it depends' if we are asked whether it is right or wrong to say something. The question 'Is it right or wrong to say what is not the case?' gives us more information but even this is not enough. We are told neither the intention in nor the consequences of saying what is not the case. So as a next step we might be asked 'Is it right or wrong to say what is not the case with the intention of setting a problem in a tutorial class?' and this additional information may enable us to answer the question. There is no single word with which we can state that someone says what is not the case with this intention. But there is a single word to state that someone says what is not the case with the intention to deceive: we use the word 'lying'. The difference then between 'Is it wrong to say what is not the case?' and 'Is lying wrong?' is that the second question does give us that additional information without which we could not answer the first question. One *could* answer the first

105

question by saying that is is not *always* wrong. What we mean by this is that we could give examples of saying what is not the case when it is right and other examples when it is wrong. The difference between the two sets of examples is that we would give different additional facts, we would describe different situations. Instances of saying what is not the case with the intention to deceive would be among the second group of examples. The word 'lying' as it were carves out for us these instances for special recognition.

Someone could object now that not only is saying what is not the case only sometimes wrong but also lying is only sometimes wrong. Without committing ourselves to a moral view let us consider the logic of this problem. According to this objection we can find examples of saying what is not the case with the intention to deceive when it is wrong and other examples when it is right. But now we do not need to give new additional facts in *both* cases. Enough has been said already by saying that the intention was to deceive, to judge it to be wrong, but this may not be the full story. If we can provide just one example when saying what is not the case with the intention to deceive is not wrong, it is enough to defeat the claim that lying is always wrong, but this would leave all *other* instances of lying still wrong. The objector might bring up the usual example of the maniac who is looking for his intended victim. His intended victim is hiding in the house but we tell the maniac that we just saw him disappear around the corner. Problems like this are sometimes represented in terms of 'conflict of principles'; we have the principle 'lying is wrong' and also 'lives ought to be saved'. Let us suppose now however that we had a single term by the help of which we can state that a life is being saved by means of a deceit. Other instances of this act could be to dress the intended victim as an old woman or to put a wardrobe in front of the door where he is hiding. We might call these instances of 'savingdeceit', and instances of savingdeceit are not instances of lying. We could apply our test of asking what one would do instead of an act of savingdeceit. One might try to ring the police or bolt the doors or frighten the maniac with a gun. If we have not got a gun to make the maniac go away we might think of another tool that can achieve the same end, we could use language. One way of making the maniac go away is by means of savingdeceit. In some cases the material elements of the notion of lying and that of savingdeceit may coincide but they amount to different acts.

To envisage such a change in our language is not a far-fetched fancy. Let me make an analogy: threat is to promise as savingdeceit is to lying in the following respect. If we did not have the term 'threat', as we now have not got the term 'savingdeceit', then we would have to use the term 'promise' to describe the action of someone who makes a threat, as now we have to use the term 'lying' to describe some acts of saving-deceit. In this case we could not unhesitatingly say that promises ought to be kept. They would not have to be kept always, and again by 'not always' we mean that we can give instances of promises when they do not need to be or should not be kept, e.g. when I promise to hit you on the head or to deprive you of a legacy. Without the term 'threat' in our language we would have to make careful distinctions between different kinds of promises by reference to their intentions and consequences, and after a more or less long description of these intentions and consequences we could say '. . . is right' or '. . . is wrong'. These judgments would not look like our 'moral principles'; they would be moral judgments. The term 'threat' carves out from the field of promises some that are made with certain intentions and have certain consequences so successfully that we do not even think that threats are promises. Since the term 'threat' covers now all those performances—among other performances—that someone could have cited as examples of promises when promises ought not to be kept, we can now freely say 'promises ought to be kept'.

If the term 'savingdeceit' performed the same function in relation to 'lie' as 'threat' does in relation to 'promise' then we would be more willing to say that lying is always wrong, or simply that lying *is* wrong. We would also now have a new 'principle': 'savingdeceit is right (or good)', and in situations where we would perform an act of savingdeceit we would no longer be confronted by a 'conflict of principles'.

Let us see now why we are inclined to call some of our moral judgments 'principles'. Out of the many uses of the term 'principle' there is a use when by asking for the principle of something we are asking for the point of that thing, for its *rationale* or for the reason why certain things are made to happen the way they do. We can ask for the principles of a machine, of a game or of selecting candidates. Editors usually explain in the Preface of their *Selections* the principles on which they included or excluded certain articles in or from the volume. In giving these principles they give their reasons for the selection, the point of view that guided their classification.

We should recall now from page 26 that the words 'right', 'wrong', 'good', 'bad' can be used as discriminators or as reminders. When a notion is not formed completely from the moral point of view (e.g. 'killing') then it includes both morally right and wrong acts and in these cases the words 'right', 'wrong' are used for selecting from a mixed class the types of acts that are different from the moral point of view. When a type of act selected completely from the moral point of view receives its own term (e.g. 'murder') then the words 'right', 'wrong' are used only as reminders, they remind us what was the point of forming such notions. I would like to call such notions complete notions.

The difference between moral judgments and 'moral principles' is that in the latter we have *complete* moral notions. Moral judgments *ex hypothesi* do not contain *complete* moral notions. This is why we have to make *judgments* by using the words 'right' or 'wrong' as discriminators and not as reminders. The formal element of a notion which is not complete does not enable us to follow a rule in such a way that only the right acts or only the wrong acts are mentioned in a series of examples of an act. The need for introducing a complete notion is precisely to effect this discrimination, as we have seen in the case of savingdeceit. Such a notion by virtue of its formal element enables us to follow a rule from the moral point of view. We can see then the sense in which a complete moral notion, by virtue of its formal element provides us with a 'principle'. Referring to a 'principle' in this sense is referring either to the formal element of an already existing complete moral notion, or to a formal element which could be the formal element of such a notion, though for some reason the notion has not been formed.

Perhaps an analogy with the often discussed example of following a rule in continuing a series of numbers may help here. When I observe someone continuing a series of numbers I may ask on what principle he is continuing the series. One may say either: 'I am giving every second number starting from number 2'; or one may give the principle by the help of a mathematical notion: 'I am giving the series of even numbers'. A moral notion can give a principle in the way in which the mathematical notion 'even' gave the principle. But the person is not giving the even numbers *on principle*, in the same way as the person who refers to a 'moral principle' does not behave *on principle*.

The sense in which a complete moral notion provides us with a principle is the sense in which it enables us to say that the following two are examples of the same act: saying what is not the case in order to bring punishment on someone for an act for which he is not responsible, and saying what is not the case in order to gain a benefit to which I am not entitled; but on the other hand saying what is not the case in order to save the life of an innocent from a maniac is not an example of the same act.

Obviously this sort of 'principle' cannot be used as a major premise in a deductive argument. Without this 'principle' we would not be able to recognize what the act is which should be stated in the 'minor premise'. But once we know what is the morally relevant description of our act we do not need a major premise to come to a conclusion.

3. THE IMPORTANCE AND VALIDITY OF MORAL PRINCIPLES

We have seen in the first two chapters that moral notions do not reflect the needs, wants, aspirations or ideals of any one person or a group of individuals, but those of anyone. This is so not because we happen to be such nice people that we formulate our notions from the point of view of anyone, but because our language is public. To presume that our notions reflect anyone's views because we are such people, or because we are fair, is to presume that our language is a private language which is turned by our benevolence into a public language. But the very notion of fairness is a notion that can exist only in our public language.

This claim does not eliminate personal decisions from our moral life, it only puts them into their proper place. Indeed, without a personal decision one's act is not a moral act. But our moral life cannot be *based* on decisions, nor our moral philosophy on the concept of decision. Without our moral notions there would be nothing to make decisions about; there would not even be a need to make decisions.

When we have to decide whether we should tell a lie in order to save someone's life, we would not be confronted by a need for a decision unless we knew that lying was wrong and that we have to save peoples' lives. Without these principles (and now that I have made clear that by 'moral principle' I mean a special type of moral judgment we can discard the inverted commas) there would be nothing to make a decision about, there would not be a need for a decision, we would not even be in a situation. It is only by the help of moral principles or other moral judgments, or at least by the help of complete or incomplete moral notions that an existentialist can produce his examples of extraordinary situations where no principle can help the moral agent to make his decision. What these extraordinary examples show is only that we have not got a single term to sum up the whole situation in which one ought to do one thing rather than another. We need a whole novel to state all the relevant facts.

The plot of such a novel could run roughly like this. Georges is condemned to death by due process of law, and Philippe, the executioner, alone knows that Georges is innocent. But Philippe also knows that Georges works for the Gestapo and is very near to discovering who are the leaders of the local resistance. We do not need to complicate the plot further; our existentialist could say that since there is no principle on which Philippe could act, he would have to make his own decision. But why would he have to make a decision at all? Would he have to make a decision at all unless he were convinced that murder is wrong? Without accepting the validity of moral principles or the force of moral notions he would not be in a complex situation. One could say that he would not be in a situation at all. He would merely be in an excellent position to dispose of a Gestapo agent.

One of the relevant facts incorporated in the notion of murder is that the murderer has no legal right to take life. Our executioner has such a legal right technically. But is he murdering all the same if he knows that the person so condemned is innocent? His problem and decision is meaningful only within our conceptual framework, which framework is not the result of his decision. Again, when he knows the man to be innocent of one crime but not of another he not only makes his decision by the help of our moral notions such as 'innocence', but he *has* to make a decision because of the force of these notions. Without the appropriateness of one or another description providing him with reasons for doing one thing rather than another he would not have to make a decision.

Let us suppose that earlier in the story Philippe was waiting in ambush for Georges who, dressed as an innocent looking farmer, was looking for the hideout of the resistance. He never came into the range of the ambush. But had he done so it would have been quite irrelevant for Philippe's decision to know that Georges was at the same time innocent of something else that he was accused of. So now in his role as an executioner he might be considering whether his act would amount to *the same* as his ambush would have amounted to. But we do not have to make the decision for him. Our aim was to show that examples of extraordinary situations can be produced only by the help of moral notions and both the predicament and the decision are intelligible only in terms of these notions. The validity of our moral principles and other moral judgments cannot be denied in these extraordinary situations because without their validity the situations would not be extraordinary. These examples are only more complex versions of the sort of problem we considered when we coined the term 'savingdeceit'. What these examples show is only what we have seen already, that there can be complex situations the relevant facts of which are not grouped together into one notion. But there is no logical reason why this could not happen. Perhaps the title of the novel could serve as a term corresponding to such a new notion. Even if it were unlikely that another example of the same situation with the same material elements would come about in the course of history there could be examples of the same situation with different material elements. In the present case another such example could be something like this. A civil servant's task happens to be to send out notices to people who have been selected for an extended overseas service. He observes that someone's name was selected by mistake. He knows however that this person is engaged in an elaborate scheme to wreck someone's marriage and nothing but his removal from the country could save that marriage.

This also illustrates the fact that moral reasoning is not deductive but analogical. Only if it were deductive should we worry about cases where there is no principle by the help of which we could deduce what to do in such and such a situation. By analogical reasoning I do not mean that we have certain paradigm cases that we know to be good or right, and then by analogy we work out what to do in similar cases. This is the view I criticized at the end of the first Chapter when I mentioned the mistake in Thomson's translation of Aristotle's theory of analogy. I pointed out there that far from knowing the meaning of 'good' already, we are trying to elucidate what it is. When we are looking for a formal element we are looking for that which alone is common to a variety of things or actions. This common element we are looking for is not one of the empirical similarities but that which brings a variety of things together as examples of the same thing. Things, happenings and situations differ from and resemble each other in many ways; what we regard as the same depends on the formal element of our notions. But sometimes the appropriate formal element is precisely what we are looking for. We can direct our attention to the appropriate formal element by trying to consider what we would or would not regard as instances of the same something. By trying to think of another instance of a situation that would be the same we are trying to think what makes the situation to be what it is. In the extraordinary situations our predicament is exactly this: we have no principle to help us because our situation has not been brought under a formal element which could enable us to form a notion of what it is. Without a notion and a term corresponding to it in our language we cannot formulate a principle. Looking for a principle is looking for a formal element.

It could be objected now that I am contradicting my earlier important claim that we can think of another example of the same thing only by the help of a formal element. Now I seem to be saying that we can find a new formal element by trying to think what other instances would be examples of the same thing. I am not saying, however, that *first* we find other instances of the same thing which will then enable us to discover the formal element; but only that the process of finding the formal element *is* the process of finding what would or would not be instances of the same thing.

Furthermore, we have seen in connection with the hierarchy of formal and material elements that some of the material elements of a notion (N1) are already organized into further formal and material elements (n2) while others are not (nx). So we may come across situations where the material elements are not organized into a notion (nx) compared to other situations (n2), but at the same time there exists a higher order notion (N1) which may help to find a new notion, may help to turn nx into one of the n2-s. We were able to make our new notion of misticket plausible only because of the existence of the notion of mistake. Or, under the notion of vice we may find murder, cruelty, etc., but these are not the only ways of being vicious. When we are in a situation that does not come under the notion of murder, cruelty or any other of these notions, we might think that our situation is without a formal element, when in fact it comes under the formal element of viciousness. So in a new situation (x) we *are* helped by a formal element in trying to find other instances of x: we are looking for that common element which would be common to our new notion (nx) *and* to murder, cruelty, etc.

It is evident that in extraordinary situations we must possess a higher order moral notion. Without that it would not be an extraordinary moral situation. From other points of view, other than the moral point of view, our situation may be the same as straightforward moral situations, or two situations that are the same from the moral point of view may not be the same from other points of view. We are in an extraordinary moral situation precisely because we have found a new fact which is relevant to the rightness or wrongness of what we are about to do. This, along with the higher formal element enables us to look for other instances of the same situation.

Our present problem then differs from Aristotle's example of analogical reasoning in two related respects. For one thing, when we are looking for a new moral notion we have already got a higher formal element that helps us in our search, or at least we have already got the highest notion in this field, the notion of right (or wrong). This must be so *ex hypothesi* because unless we viewed the situation from a moral point of view we would not have a problem. Secondly, since it is this higher order notion which makes a situation different from others, we must be in possession of two sets of *relevant* facts, the facts that make a situation different, and those that would make it standard, from the moral point of view.

If we were to think of a case when someone would have to leave his mother to join the Resistance, we would have to discern whether it is a case of leaving, forsaking, abandoning or deserting a mother. Which of these descriptions is the correct one depends on the relevant facts of the situation. If we find that none of these or any other available descriptions are appropriate, it is only because we have found some new relevant facts that would make all available descriptions inappropriate. But these new facts must be the sort or type that would be relevant for deciding between possible alternative descriptions. So the facts that would make a situation allegedly 'unique' are the sort of facts that are relevant for deciding whether a situation should or should not come under a certain description, that is, they do *not* make a situation logically unique.

A new moral situation could never be referred to by a proper name. If we used the title of a novel as a term to refer to a moral situation that title would not function as a proper name but as an expression indicating what made the situation in the novel to be what it is, that is, indicating its formal element. By being able to think of another Munich we are able to recognize what made Munich what it was, but in this case 'Munich' is not the name of a city or even the name of a situation. What in fact happened at Munich was but one example of a 'Munich'. In time it may turn out to be not even the best example.

The human activities that make it necessary for us to coin proper names make certain characteristics of people, places and events relevant for calling them by this or that proper name. But these are not the sort of facts that can be relevant for distinguishing a situation as morally different from others. The facts that can make a situation morally different are the sort that can bring a situation under some or other morally relevant description, or, which is the same, they are facts that can make it impossible to describe a situation by the available terms, and necessitate the coining of others. In this latter case, *ex hypothesi* we need a new moral notion, not a new proper name. There is a difference between introducing another Herr Quisling at a party and thinking of another Quisling.

Nevertheless, if we ask a moral agent after he has made a decision in a complex situation whether he thinks that anyone else ought to do the same, we would not be asking the empirical question whether he could visualize another situation like his or whether a situation like his would ever occur again. We would be

118

asking a question about the logic of his decision. We would be asking whether he made the decision because of his being what he is or because of the relevant facts of the situation. If he said yes, he thought that anyone else ought to do the same in that situation, he would be affirming that he based his decision on the relevant facts of the situation. His answer would not be about anybody *else*, let alone about all people, but about the dependance of his decision on the relevant facts of the situation. This is why *anybody* else in that situation ought to do the same.

Another person, however, by his presence could make a difference to the situation itself. Situations are not out there in the world, existing independently of us, so that human beings could just step in and out of them. Situations are not like puddles that we can step in and out of; to be in a situation is to be related to other human beings in a certain way.

An analysis of the notion of 'situation', which, along with other similar notions like 'predicament', is already to some extent a moral notion, would be of primary importance for a moral philosophy on a more ambitious scale than this study. Here let us only recall again that the subject matter of morals is the human beings who live that moral life, that is, who are related to each other in the relevant manner. Moral notions do not evaluate the world of description but describe the world of evaluation. As Hume observed in a way, ' "ought" expresses a new relationship'. When we turn our reflection to the relationships that exist between human beings, we turn our reflection to the area where we find moral notions. But not all human relations are relevant for our moral notions. Terms like 'situation' and 'predicament' carve out some of the relevant relationships. There is some circularity in saying that our obligations depend on the relevant facts of the situation, but this is all the more reason for the analysis of the notion of 'situation' for it would shed light on the notion of 'obligation' and on the sort of facts that are relevant for our obligations. (One should investigate for instance why one was inclined to say that if Philippe, the executioner, did not believe that murder was wrong, he would not have been in a situation but in a position, in a position to dispose of a Gestapo agent.)

It could happen that certain relationships exist between one son and his mother that do not exist between his brother and his mother, relationships that would be relevant for *anyone* who has to decide whether to leave his mother or not. It could happen that these relationships would constitute the facts that would make him to be in a situation at all. So the moral judgment I cited at the beginning of this chapter, namely: 'it is you who should stay with your mother, and your brother should join the Resistance' is not a particular judgment applicable to one person only. It is a moral judgment because anyone else in the same situation ought to do the same, that is, because the obligation depends on the relevant facts of the situation, and for this reason we can tell some- one 'it is you who ought to stay with your mother and your brother should join the Resistance'. The only difference between this moral judgment and what we may regard as moral principles is that there is no term in our language that sums up the situation in which he is.

4. 'ALWAYS GOOD' AND THE 'HIGHEST GOOD'

Earlier in this chapter when we reconstructed the notion of a lie we observed that until we were given all the relevant facts we were not able to judge the act of saying something, or even the act of saying something false, to be always right (or wrong) but only sometimes right (or wrong). A case when we can judge an act to be sometimes right is the corollary of our Argument A, according to which there must be a relevant difference between two sets of instances of the same thing if one set is good and the other is not. If these relevant facts are unspecified then we are not entitled to judge the thing good or bad, or the act right or wrong; we should say 'it depends'; that is, the rightness or wrongness of the act depends on those further specifications.

By taking away from the instances of lying those that we came to call instances of savingdeceit, that is, by further specifying the relevant facts, we made lying always wrong. If these further relevant facts entitle us to say that saying what is not the case with those facts present is wrong, then in another case with the same specifications, saying what is not the case is wrong. This is what we express by asserting that lying is always wrong. If we still think that lying is not always wrong and wish to make it so, then we have to add still further similar specifications to the notion of lying until it would be absolutely always wrong. But we have not made lying any worse than it was before, nor would an act of lying be any better if in the absence of these refinements of language we could only say that lying was sometimes wrong.

Let us say that a, b, c, d, are instances of an act X. If a and b are good while c and d are bad we can say that X is sometimes good. If by the help of two new terms we separated the first two by calling them Z while we call the second two Y, then we could say than Z is always good. But just because Z is always good, if we did Z we would not be performing a better act than if we did X when it was good to do it, for in both cases we would be doing a or b. Nor would we be any less culpable of doing either c or d if we did them under the description of X just because X is sometimes good.

The activity of moral evaluation is carried out when one considers and decides whether this or that fact is relevant to making a particular act right or wrong. When we ask by the help of a term describing an act whether the act that falls under that description is right or wrong our question is more of a theoretical kind. We are asking a question about the way in which the term specifies the act, whether it specifies the act from the moral point of view and if so to what extent. This is why judgments like 'x is always (or sometimes) good' do not further evaluate the act but say something about the logical features of our term.

To some extent these judgments are like saying that not all marbles in a bag are white. One black marble in a bag of white marbles is enough to defeat the claim than all marbles in the bag are white. Let us not be distracted by the fact that in one case we are concerned with morally good and bad acts and in this case with black and white marbles. Deciding whether an animal is carnivorous or not is a different activity from deciding whether an animal is dangerous or not. But the judgments 'not all animals are carnivorous' and 'not all animals are dangerous' have similar logical features. That judgments like 'x is not always wrong' do not seem to belong to this class may partly be due to a grammatical difference. Human acts are not identifiable particulars in the way in which animals and marbles are, so instead of 'all (or some) instances of . . .' or 'all (or some) members of the class of . . .' we more naturally employ the phrases 'always . . .' or 'sometimes . . .'

These judgments are not distributive; from 'not all marbles are white' we cannot infer that each marble is not all white, but spotted. From 'lying is not always wrong' we cannot infer that there is a bit of merit in each act of lying, or that there is some uncertainty about the rightness or wrongness of each lie. Further, the fact that not all marbles in our bag are white does not prevent us from finding in it a marble which is much whiter than any of the marbles we may find in a bag in which all marbles are white. An act of saying something that is not the case with the intention to deceive, when it is good,—if for instance it saves your brother from a maniac—may be much better than an act which is always good, like consoling a distressed child.

Let us see now the difference between our marble example and examples involving moral notions. We can enable ourselves to say that all marbles in the bag are white by picking out the black marbles from the bag. But we cannot remove bad acts from a certain field or area in a similar way. We have to make a change in our terms to 'remove' bad acts from an 'area' in order to enable ourselves to make judgments like 'x is always good'. Beside the term 'marble' we also have a bag containing the marbles, but in the case of moral terms the terms themselves function like the bags. (I am making the contrast now within this particular example; I am not claiming that only moral terms function like this.) Terms function like bags in the manner in which terms can so function, that is, not by physical but by logical means. When terms function like bags then the connection between the 'bag' and what it contains is not a contingent and empirical but a logical and conceptual relationship. So when x is a moral term, the judgment 'x is always (or sometimes) good' tells us about the logical and conceptual features of the term x; it tells us whether the term specifies an act from the moral point of view and to what extent it does this. When the term is a complete term, complete from the moral point of view, then 'right' and 'wrong' function like reminders, they signify that our term has been formed from the moral point of view. When our term is incomplete, or open to further specifications from the moral point of view, then we use 'right' and 'wrong' to discriminate and distinguish from the moral point of view between different instances of the act referred to by the incomplete term.

Towards the end of this chapter I shall argue that we do not find a highest good by finding that which is always good. In preparation for that I have to make now another obvious contrast.

There must be something wrong with a particular thing if it is only sometimes good. In some cases, as in the case of a watch, the thing would not be good at all, while in other cases it is not as good as if it were always good. When a particular thing is always good it usually possesses some special qualities for which we prefer it. A car which is always good, in other words, a reliable car, is so well constructed and is made of such materials that it never lets us down. This is the case when we talk about particular things. We have seen that in the case of human acts, that which is always good is not better than that which is only sometimes good. It is not that I am contrasting particular things with classes of acts instead of particular acts. The point is that we simply cannot even talk about particular, individual acts being sometimes or always right or good. This category of evaluation is not relevant for moral evaluation. Only when we evaluate things from the point of view of their service to us, and when these are durable things or 'goods' is it relevant to ask questions like 'how well do they serve us?', 'do they let us down?', 'are they dependable?'

To make a particular thing which is sometimes good into one which is always good we have to use a screwdriver or some other means in order to effect changes in it. To make an act which is sometimes good into one which is always good we do not exert some special effort in the performance of the act to make it better; instead, we have to specify the circumstances under which the act would be good, or provide the relevant facts that were missing from the description and without which we could not judge it to be always good.

It may be objected that we can never succeed in sufficiently specifying the intentions, results, circumstances and other relevant facts and incorporate them in one term so that using that term we could say that x is always right or wrong. But the task is not as hopeless as it may seem. Although there may be innumerable facts that one could mention in connection with anything, there are no innumerable relevant facts. To begin with, as we have already noticed, only those facts are in the running for being relevant that can make a difference to a situation. After this preselection similar other large scale eliminations reduce the number of relevant facts. Different types of situations automatically eliminate whole groups or types of facts as irrelevant. We are not confronted with an indefinite *number* of facts but with types or categories of facts and the number of these types or categories is limited. We have just observed, for instance, that the category of evaluation which evaluates durable things from the point of view of their reliability is altogether irrelevant for the moral evaluation of human acts. In this way whole areas of facts can be ignored altogether. Furthermore, a specification within one area or category can look after all the possible facts within that area. For instance, if our problem is the question of the rightness or wrongness of some form of discrimination, the area from which facts can be cited as relevant is the area of the various reasons for which someone would distinguish between human beings, and within this area only those distinctions that would result in different treatments of attitudes. Within this limited field we can specify the cases when someone does not even consider or weigh up his reasons for treating human beings differently but makes up his mind on grounds other than reasons. In fact we have a term, 'prejudice', to refer to discrimination with these specifications. Since the only field from which facts could be cited as relevant for saying that some cases

of discrimination are right is the field of one's reasons
for discrimination, and this whole field was eliminated
by one move, we can say that prejudice is always
wrong. It is possible then to create watertight terms
that can be used in judgments like 'x is always wrong
(or right)'.

As against such complete terms, open terms do not
say anything about the relevant facts in certain fields.
For instance, the notion of lying, unlike a complete
notion such as bearing false witness, does not include
anything about the purpose of deceiving. Consequently,
the presence of certain facts from this field has nothing
to do with the proper use of the term 'lying'. If we
bring up a relevant fact from this field we can still
say that the act we are performing is an act of lying,
but there are more relevant facts that have to be
considered. On the other hand, since a complete term
specifies something about the relevant facts in all the
possible fields, a new relevant fact will affect the
proper use of the term itself. Or rather, in the case of
the complete terms the only relevant facts are those
that will affect the proper use of the term. In the case
of prejudice, for instance, the only possible relevant
fact that one could bring up in order to justify one's
conduct would be good grounds for treating people
differently in a certain case, but then we can no longer
call this a case of prejudice. This is why it is possible
to say 'this is an act of lying but go ahead and do it',
but one cannot say 'this is prejudice but go ahead and
maintain it'. If we had the term 'savingdeceit' in the
way I envisaged, then the notion of a lie would include
some reference to the purpose of deceiving someone.
Deceiving someone for certain reasons would not be

called lying but engaging in savingdeceit. In this case 'lie' would function as a complete term like 'prejudice', that is, we could no longer say: 'this is an act of lying but go ahead and do it.'

Since judgments like 'x is sometimes right' are not distributive, an example of a lie which is justified by reference to further relevant facts does not invalidate the claim that lying is wrong when it is wrong. We have to distinguish however between open moral notions and non-moral notions of human acts. A human act specified by a non-moral notion can be right or wrong depending on further facts just as acts specified by an open moral notion. But in the case of non-moral notions we have to bring additional facts to make the act either right *or* wrong. In the case of a notion like lying we do not need to bring more facts to make the act wrong. An act is wrong in so far as it is an act of lying. But saying what is not the case, which is a non-moral specification of an act, is neither right nor wrong in so far as it is just saying what is not the case. To make this act either right *or* wrong we have to add further specifications. So moral notions also act like challenges. If a term which is formed from the point of view of the wrongness of an act is relevant for the description of our act, then if it is an open term, it challenges us to bring more relevant facts to justify our act, or if it is a complete term, it challenges us to bring more relevant facts that would make the term not applicable to our act. In the absence of such further relevant facts our act would be wrong irrespective of whether it is an open or a complete term which is the correct description of the act.

One can even go on to say that an act of savingdeceit *in so far as* it is an act of lying is still wrong. But we do not claim more by saying this than if we claimed that an act of lying *in so far as* it is saying what is not the case is neutral. We cannot say, however, that an act of lying is no more than just saying what is not the case, nor that savingdeceit is no more than just a lie. To condemn savingdeceit by saying that it is no more than a lie would be just as much conceptual reductionism as to condone lying by asserting that it is no more than saying what is not the case.

We cannot reduce an act to one of its material elements, we cannot say of an act that it is nothing but one or any of its material elements. But neither should we regard the material elements as means to an end. Saying what is not the case with the intention to deceive is one of the material elements of saving deceit. The relationship between formal and material elements looks like the relationship between ends and means but it should be distinguished from it, and so kept apart from the vexed problems that the question 'Does the end justify the means?' raises. In the sense in which the relationship between formal and material elements looks like a relationship of ends and means all human acts exhibit this relationship. There cannot be just a formal element existing by itself: when I perform an act I have to *do* something, I have to *use* one of the material elements to bring about the act. If I want to be kind, I have to do something that amounts to an act of kindness. So, in my example of savingdeceit I was not advocating the view that the end may justify the means.

It may be thought that another, more serious, moral consequence may be implied by some of my views. It may be assumed that according to my views we can simply redescribe our acts according to our inclinations. Furthermore, since the proper analysis of an act implies the notion of intentionality and since the agent himself can claim to know his intention in a way that nobody else can, the agent can be the final arbiter as to what he is doing.

A proper treatment of these problems would take us far outside the scope of this study and especially in to fields of philosophical psychology were most of the work is still going on. While I am aware of the complexity of these problems, the above moral implications are serious enough to call for a few brief comments to dissociate my views from these implications.

At the beginning of section 3. of this Chapter, I repeated an important theme of this study by saying that moral notions do not reflect the needs, wants, aspirations or ideals of any one person or group of individuals, but those of anyone, and then I went on to say that this does not eliminate personal decisions from our moral life. But when we make decisions we have to make them in terms of, or within the framework of, our moral notions.

A similar distinction should be made with regard to intentions. A proper analysis of a human act must involve reference to intentionality: without it we cannot give a proper description of what we are doing. But this intentionality which is built into our moral notions and which makes a difference to the proper description of an act is not the intention of any one person performing an act. When we intend to do something, or mean to do something, we can intend to do only what is describable by terms that embody references to intentionality, or, if there is no available term, we can intend to do something only if we know how our act would significantly differ from an act which is describable by our available terms. Our acts are intelligible to others as well as to ourselves only if what we intend to do is publicly describable in terms the proper use of which are governed by interpersonal rules.

The appropriateness of different descriptions cannot depend on my personal intention if I can intend only within our conceptual framework. We must therefore distinguish between the generic intentionality which is built into our terms and without which we cannot give a proper analysis of human acts, and what we may call personal intentions which are expressed in avowals like 'I meant to do such and such' or 'my intention was such and such'. So far this distinction is similar to the one we observed between decisions that are built into our terms and personal decisions that are intelligible only within the framework of these terms. But personal intentions, unlike personal decisions, are not only separated from but connected to the proper description of our acts. The proper description of an act depends on the relevant facts of the situation, and the agent's intention can feature among the relevant facts. But in so far as the agent's intention can feature among the relevant facts it must be publicly knowable or accessible, either through the agent's avowal, or through the pattern of his behaviour which makes his act intelligible and meaningful for us. For the agent himself, his intention must become the object of his reflection to form part of his assessment of what he is doing. When an appeal to a personal intention does succeed in changing the proper description of an act it succeeds by virtue of inter-personal rules that govern these procedures, and not by virtue of the fact that the agent knows what he intends to do in a way that nobody else can know it. Even if we could never be mistaken as to our own intentions, we can be mistaken as to the proper description of our act.

All this raises such complex problems that to say a little about them may be worse than to say nothing, and I referred to these problems only to indicate that my views do not imply that in our moral life we can get away with almost anything by redescribing our acts. These problems raise questions not only in the field of philosophical psychology but also in what is more specifically the field of moral philosophy. Although our avowals of personal intentions do not always succeed in changing the proper description of our act, they may succeed in excusing ourselves and sometimes in justifying ourselves. This problem would lead us to the analysis of the notion of responsibility, of the occasions on which we can say 'you should have known better', and this would raise the question why it seems to be the case that one of our fundamental obligations is to consider all the relevant facts, or rather, to consider what facts can be relevant.

We must sharply distinguish these questions from the case of the well-meaning person with good intentions. Sometimes someone may be so radically unsuccessful in doing what he ought to have done that the only thing left for us to say is that his intentions were sincere or that he had good intentions. This seems to me to be quite a different sense of 'intention' from those we were considering. Intending to do what is good is very different from having good intentions. We cannot intend to do what is good without intending to consider all the relevant facts, but we can have good intentions and be quite irresponsible.

After this digression, which was for the sake of repudiating some possible implications of my views, let us now return to some further points about our moral notions.

Some theories of ethics claim that we justify our acts by reference to intentions, while others claim that we justify them by reference to consequences. In assessing the conflicting claims of these theories it is important to remember that different terms specify relevant facts in different fields and leave facts in other fields unspecified. If a term leaves the field of consequences unspecified, then what would make the act referred to by that term right or wrong could be the consequences of that act. But this is so only because the intention has already been specified by the term. If the intention is unspecified by a term, then an act referred to by such term could seem to serve as an example supporting a theory according to which we justify our acts by reference to intentions.

There can be other reasons supporting the claims of these conflicting theories; all I wanted to do was to point out that certain examples can be adduced which while they seem to support one or the other of these theories, do not in fact do so. Complete terms, for the same reason, may appear to support an intuitionist theory of ethics. An intuitionist would claim that neither the intentions, nor the consequences, nor any other additional relevant facts are needed to judge an act or state of affairs right or wrong, good or bad: we just consider it in itself and intuit its rightness or wrongness. Of course, if a term already specifies all that we need to know to judge the act referred to by that term right or wrong, we do not need any additional relevant facts for our judgment. Such an act, which is specified by a complete term, can be said to be good in itself.

We should turn our attention now to the group of phrases: 'good in itself', 'good without qualifications' and 'unconditionally good'. I have argued already that judgments about human acts are unlike judgments about particular things in that when we judge an act to be always good we do not judge it to be any better than an act which is sometimes good. But now we have another set of judgments that give the impression that if they are applicable to an act or to a state of affairs, then that act or state of affairs is better than those to which their opposites are applicable. We may get the impression that an act which is good in itself is better than one which is not good in itself, and that an act which is good without qualifications is better than that which is good only with certain qualifications, and that what is unconditionally good is better than what is not unconditionally good. Someone may go even further than saying that these acts are better, and claim that an act or state of affairs which can be described by these terms must be the highest good or one of the highest goods. Indeed, if someone were to look for a highest good he would not settle for anything less than what can be described in these terms, and once he found such a thing, surely, he may think, he must have found the highest good. It may even be assumed that we could find the foundations of morality this way, for that which is unconditionally good must surely be the condition of all other goods.

Cases when we judge human acts good in conjunction with these phrases could be compared and contrasted with cases when these judgments do express extra evaluation; and this would be one way of showing how these phrases behave when they are applied to human acts. This is what we did when we investigated the judgment 'x is always good'. Our present problem is just an elaboration of the conclusion we came to in connection with that judgment.

When we cannot say that an act is always good we have to add some more facts to the description of the act to render it always good. So when an act is specified by a description which is incomplete from the moral point of view then we cannot say that it is good in itself. On the other hand, as I indicated when I referred to the intuitionists, an act specified by a complete term can be said to be good in itself. It is good in itself because all that we need to know in order to judge it good is incorporated in the term that specifies that act in question. The same is true about 'good without qualification' and 'unconditionally good'. We have to give further qualifications to an incomplete description or specify certain conditions in order to be able to judge these acts always good. Once these qualifications and/or conditions are incorporated in a term then an act referred to by that term can be said to be good without qualification or unconditionally good. We have seen, however, that an act which is describable by a complete term may not be as good as an act whose description requires a host of qualifications. So these judgments are not about the merits or value of our acts but about the logical features of the terms that we use in talking about our acts.

Because this attempt to find the highest good is so simple in structure, we should not be misled into thinking that we will not encounter it in more sophisticated theories. But if I am right in saying that the difference between that which is always and that which is sometimes good is not one of degree in value but a degree of specification, then we cannot find the highest good by trying to find that which is always good, and so, good in itself, good without qualification or unconditionally good. Still less can we go on to make the assumption that that which is unconditionally good is the condition of all other goods, or that everything receives its goodness from that which does not receive its goodness from anything else. (That which is sometimes good, or not good in itself, 'receives' its goodness from something else, namely, from the further specification. But had our term incorporated that specification to begin with, while leaving something else unspecified, then the act referred to by that term would 'receive' its goodness from something else.)

At the same time, the simplicity of my argument should not make us think that the various systems of ethics that try to find the highest good boil down to nothing else than the erroneous move I pointed out. Plato would come to one's mind as a most obvious example of someone who might have argued the way I indicated, since he regarded only what is always good as good, just as he regarded only what is always true as true. And yet he was the first to point out that the solution of these problems lies in the art of proper divisions. These divisions should follow the 'objective articulations; we are not to attempt to hack off parts like a clumsy butcher'. (*Phaedrus* 265 e. Hackforth's translation). The Sophists were able to give the impression that the same thing is like and unlike, one and many, and also that the same act is both right and wrong, good and bad, because they did not realize that they were talking about many things under the same term, some of which were this sort, others of that sort. The whole of the *Phaedrus*, for example, is an exercise to demonstrate this. Plato tries to show there that two speeches describing the characteristics of love came to different conclusions, one to the conclusion that love is good, the other that love is bad, because we group together under one form, under the form of love, or 'irrationality' as it is defined in the dialogue, things that are different from the point of view of good and bad. It is not the case that the two speeches were about different things, they were both about love. Many different things can be the *same* in so far as they are instances of love, but at the same time they may not be the same under different formal elements. This is precisely what causes the confusion that the *same* thing is both this and that, as in this case both good and bad. So, according to Plato, after the first stage of his procedure, 'in which we bring a dispersed plurality under a single form', the second stage is 'the reverse of the other, whereby we are enabled to divide into forms, following the objective articulation', whatever we grouped together under one form.

To take example from our two recent speeches. The single general form which they postulated was irrationality; next, on the analogy of a single natural body with

K

its pairs of like-named members, right arm or leg, as we say, and left, they conceived of madness as a single objective form existing in human beings. Wherefore the first speech divided off a part on the left, and continued to make divisions, never desisting until it discovered one particular part bearing the name of 'sinister' love, on which it very properly poured abuse. The other speech conducted us to the forms of madness which lay on the right-hand side, and upon discovering a type of love that shared its name with the other but was divine, displayed it to our view and extolled it as the source of the greatest goods that can befall us. (266a.)

To assume that love is both good and bad is the same sort of assumption as to assume that the human arm or leg is both left and right. Not each arm is both left and right, some are left, some are right. But since they are all grouped together under a term which was not formed from the point of view of left and right, they can be left or right and still be arms. Similarly, not each instance of love is both good and bad; some are good, some are bad. Some, with certain specifications, may be very good indeed. In fact one is able to find under the description 'irrational behaviour', which *cannot* be said to be *always* good, behaviour which can be extolled 'as the source of the *greatest* goods that can befall us'.

If Plato, who would come to one's mind most readily as someone who might have fallen into the error of finding the highest good by finding that which is always good, did not make this error, then *a fortiori* one cannot assume that my argument undermines systems of ethics that are suspect of this error. My aim was only to bring to our attention certain moves that we may or may not make in the limited field of moral arguments that are connected with moral notions.

Aristotle, for one, did think that Plato committed this error, if he was referring to Plato in 1096 b. of the *Nicomachean Ethics*:

> . . . If we are allowed to argue on these lines, we shall find no difference either between the really good and the good, in so far as both are good. Nor will the really good be any more good by being 'eternal'. You might as well say that a white thing which lasts a long time is whiter than one which lasts only a day.'

Although in my marble example I also used colours for comparison, there is a difference in Aristotle's criticism. I pointed out that 'always' in the case of acts does not refer to duration but corresponds more to the phrase 'all instances of'. Because 'always' does not refer to duration in the case of acts, to judge them always good is not an extra evaluation. Certainly a white thing which lasts longer is not whiter than one which lasts for a day. But a car which lasts longer would be better than one which lasts only for a day. But since we do not evaluate human acts from the point of view of their duration, this sort of evaluation is irrelevant for human acts. So to bring home the argument to the field of acts, in my example of the marbles I asked 'Is a marble less white if it is classified with black marbles?' and not 'Is a marble less white if it lasts only for a short time?'. But Aristotle's way of arguing may be more appropriate if Plato thought of his Forms in terms of duration.

These problems are applicable not only to actions

and dispositions but also to states of affairs. In G. E. Moore's *Principia Ethica* the candidates for the position of the highest good, or goods, are states of affairs and not actions. The problems involved however are the same. In looking for *the* good he is looking for that which is always good, he is looking for states of affairs that are good in themselves in the sense that they are always and unconditionally good. He is conducting this search in terms of 'organic wholes' in such a way that the addition of various elements to an 'organic whole' will render it good in itself. Instead of adding qualifications to the description of an act he adds qualifications to the description of states of affairs. I am referring of course to the last Chapter of *Principia Ethica*, though the procedure itself is described already in the second half of the first Chapter.

It is interesting to note that the reason why Moore's candidates for the highest goods are states of affairs and not actions or a certain type of will or disposition is already due to the problem of judging something to be always good. Moore takes the position from the very start (*Principia*, pp. viii–ix.) that actions can be judged good or bad only by reference to the results of the action in question, and since these judgments involve what he calls 'causal truth', we can never be certain of the rightness or wrongness of our acts. 'Indeed, so many different considerations are relevant to its truth or falsehood [i.e. truth or falsehood concerning the results of the action], as to make the attainment of probability very difficult, and the attainment of certainty impossible' (p. viii). If actions are right or wrong in so far as they *may or may not* produce certain things or states of affairs then obviously the candidates for what we can judge to be always good must come from the field of things and states of affairs. Were we to construct a theory according to which things or states of affairs are right or wrong in so far as they create certain dispositions in us or help us to have a good will or to perform good acts, then we may not be able to judge states of affairs always good or good in themselves. So the reason why actions cannot even be candidates for the position of the highest good in Moore's ethics is that the place he allocates to actions in his system renders it impossible to judge actions to be always right or good.

It would be foolish to attempt a closer examination of the various systems of ethics from the point of view of the method by which they arrive at the highest good. To do them justice would involve us in complex arguments. We can find however two paragraphs in Professor Paton's commentary on Kant's *Groundwork* which formulate our problem briefly. Though I am quoting Paton's words out of their context, I quote them only because this is the most concise passage I know which illustrates how the search for the highest good is often conducted in terms of and by the help of the expressions I briefly discussed.

If a good will is the only thing which is an unconditioned or absolute good in the sense that it must be good in every possible context, can we go on to assert with Kant that it must therefore be the highest good?

The phrase 'highest good' is ambiguous. It may mean merely the good which is itself unconditioned and is the condition of all other good. In this sense 'highest good' and 'absolute good' mean precisely the same thing. But Kant is also making a judgment of value; for such a good is to be *esteemed* as 'beyond comparison higher' than any other good. Its usefulness or fruitlessness can neither add to, nor subtract from, this unique and incomparable worth.' (*The Categorical Imperative*, p. 41.)

As a natural conclusion to this chapter one cannot help making a few general remarks about various systems of ethics, for, as we observe, the logic of moral notions is central to all of them.

An intuitionist is able to intuit an obligation in a situation only if the situation is described by a moral term which is complete; a deductive system can have major premisses only if the crucial term in the major premiss is a complete moral term; a utilitarian can have a highest good only if that highest good is described by a complete term; a positivist can claim that words like 'wrong' add nothing significant to our judgment if what we judge to be wrong is described by a complete moral term, and the existentialist can claim that principles are no help in one's moral decisions only if the situation is such that it cannot be described by the help of a complete moral term.

The logic of complete moral notions also explains how these systems succeed in their various ways in distilling all value from our ordinary life and language, leaving them empty of value, concentrating it into a 'purely evaluative element'. For an intuitionist like Prichard the consideration of facts is not a moral activity but is like any other empirical consideration: the moral act is the act of intuition. The positivists only substitute an expression of attitude towards, in place of an intuition about, something which they

142

think can be empirically ascertained. In other systems the 'purely descriptive' statement of our acts takes either the form of a minor premiss with which our obligation is deductively connected via a major premiss, or the form of a causal statement with which our obligation is causally connected *via* a highest good. The existentialists are no exception and provide another variation of this pattern. Their world is without values and the purely evaluative element is there in the claim that we create values by our decisions. We have seen that what is created in these situations is that formal element in the absence of which there could not be a complete moral term.

The purely evaluative element in a world in which otherwise there is no value reminds one of what Marx said about money. Without agreeing with his observation I quote it in order to be able to make use of it. 'Money is the universal, independently constituted value of all things. It has, therefore, deprived the whole world, both the world of man and nature, of its own value. Money is the alienated essence of man's work and his being' (MEGA 1/1, p. 603).

It is the 'purely evaluative element' of our moral philosophy which is the universal, independently constituted value of all things which has therefore deprived the whole world, both the world of man and nature, of its own value. The 'evaluative element' is the alienated essence of man's work and his being.

CHAPTER FIVE

EVALUATION AND MORAL NOTIONS

IT is an interesting phenomenon that we tend to expect that a contribution to moral philosophy, more than a contribution to any other branch of philosophy, will give us the answers to all the major problems within its field. This expectation takes a subtle form. It is not that if someone deals with problems within a limited area we expect him to deal with other problems as well, but we expect those arguments, at the same time, to be arguments about other problems as well. If someone deals with, say, the inference patterns exhibited in moral arguments, we are tempted to regard his conclusions as telling us what is the distinguishing feature of moral arguments and also what is the foundation of morality, what is the distinction between right and wrong, and what is the highest good. The answers to the same set of problems are expected from a contribution to another limited field, say, from a contribution to the study of the various uses of the word 'good'. While a work may be at least an illuminating contribution in a limited field, it may easily be dismissed for not providing the right answers to these other large problems.

It is not therefore out of modesty that I want to say that this present study does not deal with any of the major problems of moral philosophy. Nor is it that I want to point out this obvious fact before any of my readers do so. What I have to emphasize is not that questions like: 'what is the foundation of morality?' or 'what is the moral point of view?' and many others have not been answered or treated in the preceding pages, but that what I had to say in these pages should not be regarded as answers to these questions. It might be argued that I should have discussed or at least indicated what the moral point of view is, besides discussing some of the logical features of those notions that are formed from this point of view. But I am anxious that what I had to say about the logical features of these notions should not be mistaken for an answer to the question 'what is the moral point of view?'

In fact, part of my effort was devoted to trying to show that the logical features of moral notions cannot provide us with the answer to this question, nor can they tell us what distinguishes moral from other notions. The logic of moral notions exhibits essential similarities to non-moral notions. This of course does not eliminate the distinction between moral and other notions, it only shows that we find this difference elsewhere, namely in the reasons for forming the different notions.

Not even the fact that moral notions are formed from a particular point of view distinguishes them from other notions, because all notions are formed for some reason and from some point of view. Even when we make our notions follow patterns given by nature, as in botany or geology, we do so because there is a point in doing so. Far more is this the case in the field of some of the other sciences, where we form notions in order to be able to make predictions or to be able to control things. Then in our everyday life the notion of 'function', which is a very high order notion consisting almost entirely of a formal element, guides the formation of a large variety of lower order notions until we get down to such low order functional terms as medicine, furniture, fertilizer, etc. It would be impossible to find the descriptive point of view among all the points of view that guide the formation of our notions. In fact my view is that whenever we use a term composed of formal and material elements we describe—but never from the descriptive point of view. It does not follow from this that we can never know the facts, only that we always want to know the facts for some reason. This is what puts moral notions alongside all other notions. In all cases we group together certain facts about the world or ourselves or our activities, but in different cases we do this for different reasons and with different consequences. We describe the inanimate world for various different reasons, and ourselves and our activities for various different reasons. So 'descriptive term' cannot be used in contrast to other terms, though if we could determine what could properly be called the 'descriptive point of view', that could be used in contrast to other points of view. In this case we would have description from the descriptive as well as from the predictive, functional, moral, prudential, etc., points of view. The problem therefore is not what the difference is between descriptive and moral notions but what is the difference between describing from the moral, as against other, points of view.

Besides the similarities, we have also observed an important difference between moral and other notions, but again I must emphasize that this difference does not provide us with the moral point of view any more than the similarities did. I intend to summarize this difference and then to outline a further problem which this will lead us to, *viz.* the problem of the difference between evaluation and moral notions.

The difference between moral and other notions, I have already argued, is that moral notions are not only formed by ourselves but they are also about ourselves. This statement is imprecise in two respects. Some of the other notions are also about ourselves in so far as we are part of the physical or organic world, while moral notions are about ourselves in so far as we are rule-following rational beings. But there are also other notions that are about ourselves in so far as we are rule-following rational beings, like 'clever', 'consistent', 'learned', etc., which are not necessarily moral notions. While it is easy to eliminate the first group, the delineation of moral notions from the second group would require an investigation of the moral point of view. Since such an investigation is not our concern here, I leave it at this, that we find moral notions among those that we form about ourselves in so far as we are rule-following rational beings.

This difference between moral and other notions, we remember, had important consequences, which could be summarized by saying that (*a*) moral notions have to be public twice over: they not only have to be formed from the point of view of anyone, but they also have to be about those features of our lives that can be the feature of anyone's life; (*b*) they provide not only the rules for our thinking about the world but also the rules for our behaviour, while other notions are not at the same time rules for the behaviour of their subject matter; (*c*) partly as a consequence of (*b*), if other notions did not exist those events that are their subject matter would still go on happening, but without moral notions there would be nothing left of their subject matter.

These points have far reaching consequences for the logical behaviour of moral notions. Here I just want to draw our attention to the fact that moral judgments, far from being expressions of attitudes, emotions, likes or dislikes towards empirically observable entities or happenings in the world (which are usual candidates for the subject matter of 'descriptive statements') do not express even different, more rational judgments or evaluations of the inanimate world. They are simply not about that world. So the picture which would suggest that 'descriptive statements' state how things are and moral judgments express our atitudes, decisions or even evaluations of that world is not so much a misleading picture as not the picture of anything. Nor is it the case that moral judgments express our attitudes, decisions or even evaluations of a different world, the world of our interpersonal life, for without moral notions there would be nothing to express an attitude to, nothing to make a decision about, nothing to evaluate. So judgments made by the use of moral notions, that is, moral judgments, cannot be expressions of attitudes towards, or even evaluations of, something, if by these very notions we state what the attitudes, evaluations are supposed to be about.

The proper field of the activity of evaluation is not the world of our moral life. (For a more proper treatment of these problems one should investigate the full implications of the fact that evaluation as well as description is an activity.) I would like to mention three activities that can be candidates for the activity of evaluation and then say that only the third one is what is specifically evaluation.

(1) It is sometimes thought that if in response to a claim like 'this is murder' we ask for a description of what has happened, we are contrasting evaluation with description. But this is parallel to any request when we want to know whether a thing, happening or act has properly been described. If someone claims that a substance is fertilizer, or that we are experiencing an anticyclone the same request can be made by asking for a 'description'. We are not asking for a 'description' in these cases as against an 'evaluation', but we are enquiring whether those material elements are present that entitle us to use a certain term. We are not asking for something 'neutral' as against something 'evaluative', but we are asking for the relevant facts. When we are asked to describe the substance which we claim to be fertilizer, we are not asked to describe the substance differently, e.g. 'it is a brown powdery stuff', but to establish the correctness of our original *description*. When we are asked to describe what we claim to be murder, we are not asked to substitute a different description, e.g. 'he moved his arm very fast', but to substantiate our *original descrip-*

tion. Since what we are asked to do is to give that description on which we can base our claim, we are not asked to give such a description on the basis of which one could not claim that the substance was fertilizer or that the act was an act of murder. Only if the claim cannot be substantiated can one demand a *different description.* But equally, if the original description had been 'he moved his arm very fast', we might end up by saying 'he murdered someone', after having been asked for a proper description. We met this problem earlier when we noted that one can break the rules for the proper use of terms with regard to material as well as formal elements. This problem is present whenever we use terms consisting of material and formal elements.

(2) The second activity which may be thought of as an activity of evaluation is a version of this. It is sometimes thought that when I say 'this is a table' I am describing, but when I deliberate whether this is a table or something else then I am evaluating. Here we are concerned again with the question of proper description and these problems arise when we find that some of the material elements are not present, or other material elements are present which make the object or event in question exhibit similarities to other objects or events. When we met this sort of problem in connection with the existentialist-type decisions we noted that two factors help us resolve these problems: (*a*) we must be aware of and in possession of not only the facts but the relevant facts, because *ex hypothesi* the problem arises because of new facts that we regard as relevant; (*b*) we have the

formal elements to help in our decision because if we did not know what the facts are relevant to and did not know for what reason we wanted the proper description, our problem would not even arise.

Since a statement of the material elements never entails a statement of what the thing in question is, there is a decision in claiming what a thing is even in the standard, let alone in the borderline cases. In all cases it is the formal element which enables us to follow a rule, enables us to decide what should or should not be regarded as instances of 'the same'. So this second candidate for the activity of evaluation is a variation of the first, being concerned with the proper description of the world; and its problems are present whenever we use terms composed of formal and material elements.

There can of course be cases when something could be either a this or a that without any relevant facts helping us to make a decision. There may not even be a reason why it should matter whether we say that it is a this or a that, and the only reason why we should make a decision is because we have to say something. I do not know whether this would be a case of making a decision but it is certainly not a case of evaluation. Tossing a coin is not evaluation.

(3) The proper field of the activity of evaluation is not, as in the previous two cases, when we have to decide about alternative descriptions but when we have to decide about the qualities of particulars falling under one and the same description. We always evaluate under a certain description. We judge something to be a good such and such. Other constructions

and phrases using the word 'good' fall into the pattern of 'a good such and such' with one notable exception, when 'good to . . .' is used meaning good towards and not good with an infinitive. In this case we are not saying that someone or something is a good instance of a such and such but are talking about human relationships that can bring us back to the field of morals.

We do not use the phrase 'good for' when the object *is* for what we would want to judge it good for. We do not say that telephones are good for ringing up people or that shoes are good for protecting our feet. Not because they are not good for these but because these are what they are for. Only when it was being explained for the first time what they were for could perhaps the phrase 'good for' be used. We can say however that telephones are good for, say, keeping the door open. We use the phrase 'good for' when we use something for what it is not for, when we want to evaluate something under a *different description*, e.g. in this case *good as* a doorstop. The phrase 'good as' should be followed by a description, and the phrase indicates under what description we are evaluating something. Sometimes no single term exists for a new description and this may obscure the fact that all these phrases conform to the pattern of 'a good such and such'. To evaluate skills we use the phrase 'good at'. If the skill in question can be described by the use of one phrase we can evaluate someone's skill by saying that he is a good such and such, e.g. that he is a good carpenter. In the absence of a term like, e.g. 'firelighter' we say that he is good at lighting fires. 'Good to . . .' when it is followed by a verb, falls into the same pattern: what is good to eat is good as food or as nourishment.

This evaluation, when we evaluate particulars falling under a description should not be confused with *valuing* things for what they are. We value tables and medicines, as against earthquakes and measles. To say that tables are good things is different from saying that this is a good or bad table, and to say that earthquakes are bad is different from saying that this is a good or bad earthquake. One way of making the distinction is to say that we can evaluate particulars as good or bad instances of a such and such, but then we also value or detest, seek or avoid or are indifferent to things in so far as they are such and such. In the first case I said we *evaluate*, in the latter that we *value* (or detest, etc.) things in so far as they are such and such. In the latter case we do not need to evaluate. In cases when we value or detest something in so far as it is a such and such we do so because we formed the notion of a such and such from the appropriate point of view. We form notions from other points of view than those of valuing or detesting, seeking or avoiding certain things but my observation applies generally. In cases when we are indifferent to things in so far as they fall under a certain description we have no reason to value or avoid them under that description, otherwise we would have formed different notions of them. Of course we can further evaluate things under a different description, and this is when we use phrases like 'good as . . .' or 'good for . . .' We can evaluate even pebbles by saying that they are good as ballast or good for cobblestones. Here we do not evaluate them in so far as they are pebbles but as instances of ballast or paving material. What happens in these cases is that something which is already specified by a term is brought under another term as a particular of that other term. Although it retains its original description we are not evaluating it under that, but as a particular under another description. Without a certain description we cannot evaluate anything. But we do not evaluate descriptions, but particulars by reference to or by the help of certain descriptions. The terms themselves by the help of which we describe something are formed from certain points of view, and this is why evaluation here is either redundant or irrelevant. It is redundant if the reason for forming a notion was that we value certain things, and irrelevant if the reason for forming a notion is not that we value, seek or want to avoid certain things. In the latter case *ex hypothesi* there is no point in evaluating something in so far as it comes under a 'neutral' description.

Needless to say there is a close logical connection between description and the evaluation of particulars falling under the description. The formal element of a notion determines what are the relevant qualities falling under a description, and we judge particulars to be good or bad by reference to their qualities relevant to the description, so it follows that the formal element of a notion is logically connected to the evaluation of particulars. Nevertheless, we must distinguish between the two roles of the formal element: first its role in determining what type of notion we have, and secondly its role in determining what are the relevant qualities of a particular for judging it a good such and such. These two roles might diverge with regard to valuing and evaluating. We do not value burglars but we can evaluate someone as a good burglar, and in the previous chapter we observed that the original events of Munich which gave rise to the notion of a Munich, may turn out in time not to be the best instance of a Munich.

The evaluation of particulars is possible not because we value something in so far as it falls under a description but because the description functions like a standard to which particulars approximate. We saw in the first chapter that no term can be reduced to a statement of, or an enumeration of, its material elements. This also means that we can never equate or identify what we say a thing is with any of its instances or examples, and that *all* observable particulars are instances or examples of what they are. I am claiming that apart from such exceptional cases like the standard metre in Paris, there are no paradigm particulars, but rather that, as a supposed paradigm case would serve as a standard for other particulars, our notions of things serve as standards for all the respective particulars that come under them. The various particulars exemplify more or less what they are supposed to be under a certain description. It is by virtue of this fact that we can evaluate them.

We also observed, when we discussed the alleged uniqueness of existentialist-type situations that there must be more than one instance of anything which can be described by the help of a term consisting of formal and material elements. Evaluation is possible only when there are or can be more than one instance of a thing. If something were unique in the sense that we could refer to it only by a proper name, say, Jack, then we could not say that it was or was not a good Jack. Of course we could still evaluate Jack under a description by saying that Jack was good for putting things on or good as Hamlet (Hamlet is not a proper name here but a role that can be played by different actors), but in these cases we are not evaluating Jack as Jack. The reason why it is a prerequisite of evaluation that there should be more than one instance of a thing is not that we need several instances for comparison. Even if as an empirical fact there is but one instance of a thing, it must be described by a term of which logically there could be more than one instance in order that we should be able to evaluate it. We can evaluate something as an x only when x tells us what the thing is supposed to be, and this can be done only by a description. Descriptions, unlike proper names, can provide standards. It is significant the philosophers who claim that in the world there is no value attempt to 'describe' that world by a process more akin to naming than describing. The dichotomy between description and evaluation should be called the dichotomy between naming and evaluation.

Another distinction must now be made before we can return to moral notions. We must distinguish between the many particular instances of a thing when these instances are particulars in the world of space and time, and the many instances of higher order notions when these instances are other notions. The proper field of evaluation is the field of particulars in the world of space and time, and only in very theoretical discussions do we occasionally evaluate notions as instances of higher order notions. Although a higher order notion has several instances of lower order notions, this relationship is radically different from the relationship between a notion and its particular instances in the spatio-temporal world. The relationship between the notion of furniture and its instances such as the notions of table and wardrobe is different from the relationship between the notion of a table and particular tables. Again, the relationship between the notion of viciousness and its instances such as the notions of murder or cruelty is different from the relationship between the notion of murder and particular acts of murder. Only in theoretical discussions would we say that tables and chairs are good instances or examples of furniture, but this is not why we value tables and chairs.

If we turn now to moral judgments we should observe that in our moral life we are not evaluating. We may be performing one of the first two activities that I considered as possible candidates for the activity of evaluation but not the third. That is to say, we may be concerned in one way or another with the proper description of situations or acts but we are not concerned with evaluation. Of course one is performing particular acts in one's moral life, but when I ask whether I should do this or that, by 'this' or 'that' I mean acts of *different descriptions* and not this or that particular act that fall under the same description. When one makes a moral decision one does not choose the good instance of an act that falls under a certain description but works out the proper description of the situation on the basis of the relevant facts, and understands the significance of the description. As we have just seen, with regard to descriptions evaluation is either redundant or irrelevant. If the proper description of a situation involves moral notions, notions formed from the moral point of view, then evaluation is redundant. If the proper description of a situation does not call for moral notions then evaluation is *ex hypothesi* irrelevant. There can sometimes be a further problem of choosing the particular manner in which one should bring about an act of a certain description but this is not the moral problem, unless in some exceptional cases this raises the question whether the end justifies the means.

The fundamental differences between evaluation and moral judgments did not prevent us from seeing a core of similarity between them, but this similarity is exhibited not only between them but between all rational human activities that make use of language.

When we evaluate something we can make the following three assertions about our evaluation:

(*a*) If I say: '*x* is good' I cannot say '*y* is exactly the same as *x* except that *y* is not good; this is the only difference between them', because there is no extra quality or property called 'good'.

(*b*) If I say '*x* is good', I cannot say '*y* is exactly the same as *x* but *y* is not good', because in this case I cancel my reasons for saying that *x* is good.

(*c*) If I say '*x* is good' I must be able to say that *any* *x* which has the same relevant qualities or properties as *x* is also good, because we judge *x* to be good for having those qualities or properties.

Parallel to these we can make the following three assertions about our moral judgments:

(*a*) If I say: 'In situation *x* I ought to do *A*' I cannot say 'Situation *y* is exactly the same as situation *x* except that in *y* I ought not to do *A*; this is the only difference between them', because there is no extra property called 'obligation'.

(b) If I say 'In situation x I ought to do A' I cannot say 'Situation y is exactly the same as x but in situation y I ought not to do A', because in this case I would cancel my reasons for my obligation in situation x.

(c) If in situation x I ought to do A then *anybody* else in a situation which is the same as x in all relevant respects also ought to do A, because my obligation depends on the situation and not on the fact that I am I.

These assertions however can be made about any rational activity that makes use of language; we can, for instance, make these three assertions about judging something to be a tulip. But these very same rules have different consequences and implications in the different fields of our rational activities: when we engage in everyday conversation, when we do science, when we evaluate things and when we act as moral agents. We can observe, for instance, in the above parallel assertions that while the goodness of something depends on the relevant qualities or properties of things, our obligations depend on the relevant facts of situations. In the third parallel, (c), we can observe that this results in the one case in the fact that our judgment applies to *any thing* that has the same qualities or properties, in the other case in the fact that our judgment applies to *any one* who is in the same situation. A further consequence of this is that while in the case of evaluation I am bound to make the same *judgment* when the same qualities or properties are present, in the case of our moral life the same rules of rationality result in my being under the same *obligation* as anyone else when I am in a certain situation. In order to arrive at this practical conclusion about anyone as against a theoretical conclusion about any thing, we do not need to turn to additional rules of rationality but to a different field of the application of the same rules of rationality. Whatever may be the merits of practical syllogisms, their major premisses cannot be merely evaluative judgments whether about dry foods or juicy strawberries. An evaluative premiss about the inanimate world can result in an evaluative conclusion but only a description of a situation can result in my being under an obligation.

I am aware that these, like some of my earlier conclusions, may sound paradoxical. But when one argues against a theory in a terminology which itself embodies the very theory one is arguing against, paradoxical remarks cannot be avoided. Right through this study I have been using the terminology of contemporary moral philosophy like a Wittgensteinian ladder. Some of these ladders I surreptitiously threw away on the way but others I have had to use right to the end. I hope I shall be forgiven for the inevitable paradoxical remarks. This is also one of the conclusions that can be drawn from this study, that it is very difficult to question some of the prevailing theories and doctrines of our moral philosophy because they have shaped our terminology and are embodied in it. When we think we question these theories we merely ask a question within the theories, and so each attempt to question them only reaffirms them. We not only look through a frame that we do not notice but since in this case the frame creates what we are discusing, we are only looking at the frame, and this is what we do not realize.

What I have been trying to say in this study is that moral notions do not evaluate the world of description; we evaluate that world by the help of descriptive notions. Moral notions describe the world of evaluation. If this sounds strange, then we have become aware of the framework within which contemporary moral philosophy moves.

INDEX

163